Mantis

Mantis

A Journal of Poetry, Criticism & Translation Issue 21

Mantis

A Journal of Poetry,
Criticism & Translation

Issue 21

2023

Editor-in-Chief
Jason Beckman

Managing Editor
Katherine Whatley

Editors
Jonathan Atkins
Lorenzo Bartolucci
Gilad Shiram

Guest Editor for Exchanging Cups:
Contemporary Sake Poetry
Kazuyo Fukao

Advisory Board
Marisa Galvez
Cintia Santana
Kenneth Fields
Roland Greene
Laura Wittman

ISSN 1540-4544

Mantis publishes poems,
translations, interviews, and
critical prose about poetry and
poetics. Each issue features
one or more clusters of work
engaging a particular theme,
writer, or question.

Orders & Submissions
For information about
submissions and to order copies
of this or previous issues of
Mantis, please visit our website:
mantis.stanford.edu

Mantis Journal
Pigott Hall, Bld. 260
450 Jane Stanford Way
Stanford, CA 94305

mantispoetry@stanford.edu

Cover: Photograph by
Kazuyo Fukao (front) with
AI watercolor by
Jason Beckman (back)

Design
Joshua Edwards
www.architecturefortravelers.org

Printed and bound by
CPI Group (UK) Ltd,
Croydon, CR0 4YY

Mantis 21 is made possible by a grant from the Research Unit in the Division of
Literatures, Cultures, and Languages.

CONTENTS

INTRODUCTION TO *MANTIS 21*

Mantis enters its third decade.

And for our next trick, we're flipping the script. For as long as we've been around, *Mantis* has aimed to bring the best in new poetry and poetry in translation into print, mostly in that sequential order. An ordering that, I must note, is not meant to place any greater value or emphasis on poetry written in English than poetry written in every other language. Still, as a translator and scholar who works primarily on literature not in English, I can't help but pause at the conjunction. Poetry *and* translation. Embedded in the words, a temporality, a primacy of that which comes before, as time (and text) ambles from the left, rightward.

Yet, sequences set not in stone be.

With some truly stellar translated poetry collaborations arranged by our editors, we dedicate this issue to the art of translation, to the care taken to transform words written in one language into poetry in another, and to the vital ambition of the translator who is compelled to engage in such a labor of love.

The issue begins with "Exchanging Cups," a special section of tanka poetry written on the theme of sake, coordinated by editor Katherine Whatley in collaboration with our friends at Hirano Jozo Sake Brewery in Gifu Prefecture, Japan. The title page of the issue features an image of the *sakagura* during the brewing process, and the cover returns us back to the days of harvest under the wide blue skies of late summer. Stretching onto the back cover, we extended the image with a bit of AI editing magic to create a bridge between our cultures, blending the rice fields quite uncannily with a landscape suggestive of the vineyards of the California coast.

Whether you're an aficionado of the traditional Japanese beverage or have never tasted it, the poems we've collected are sure to rouse a certain longing in every reader, and might just leave you thirsty for more. Following the sake poetry, I thought it fitting to put out a call asking poets for their odes to their own spirits, a pick-your-poison adventure that "raises a glass"–*kanpai, saúde, cin cin*—from one corner of the earth to another.

Transitioning into our translation section proper, this year we're featuring work by poets and translators working in ten different languages, ranging from classical Japanese to modern Greek, spanning five continents. Somehow, across the expanses of space and time in which these distinct pieces were composed, there is an airy, almost dreamlike quality that links them, lulling us as readers into a kind of profound awakening.

To conclude our spotlight on translation, we turn to the voices of two poets from Ukraine who, as editor Lorenzo Bartolucci expresses in his eloquent introduction, remind us of poetry's power to interrogate history and ask us, in the same breath, to critically remember. Now as ever, it is our duty to listen.

And if, in the end, your appetite for poetry isn't quite sated by these offerings, it just so happens that we conclude this issue with one of our most massive collections of new poetry to date. It was a record year for submissions and we have chosen to share as much of the excellent poetry we received as we possibly could. I've already lost count of the number of poets who grace this year's issue, and giving an overview of the stunning range of style and content would be near impossible. So, simply, I will make no attempt.

Instead, I offer this rumination:

In many ways, a poem is like a cocktail. For each of us exists a perfect balance of flavor to tickle our fancy—be it a certain rhyme or meter, an ineffable flow, a turn of phrase that lingers on the back of the tongue, the lilting lull of a caesura, pristinely positioned. Sometimes it's that acerbic assonance we seek, thick with bitters, an alcoholic gut-punch with a burn that slides all the way to the heart of things. Or maybe it's clean, simple, with well-defined edges, with a non-alcoholic spirit base but no less complex (there's a little something for everyone here). But a great poem, like a great cocktail, is one that stays with us. That with its scent and flavor has the power to bring us back to a moment in time, to where we were, to who we were with—to who we were, then and now. So here's to you, reader. I wish unto you the hours that poetry will bring, filled to the brim, mind runneth over. Linger on those words that catch you, swirl their sound and image around and enjoy the bouquet before you take your next sip. Settle in, and savor.

Jason Beckman
Editor-in-Chief

EXCHANGING CUPS: CONTEMPORARY SAKE POETRY

Asahi Chiyo

Ayabe Bokusui

Bonkuranaosu

Brewer Poet

Goto Noriyuki

Goto Susumu

Hanada Atsuko

Hara Hiroko

Hayakawa Michiko

Hojo Koyomi

Hoshihara Fudo

Keigetsu

Kimura Hiroshi

Kiuchi Miyuki

Kondo Yoshihiro

Mabuchi Sadazou

Masaki Rika

Murakami Atsushi

Murakami Hideo

Nagahata Takanori

Nakamura Sayoko

Nishibe Minoru

Nishiguchi Akiko

Nogami Taku

Okumura Toshio

Okuyama Isao

Onogi

Otsuka Miho

Sadao

Sato Saiichiro

Soejima Kimiyo

Sugimoto Keiji

Tanaka Tetsuo

The Dancing Veganista

Yoshimura Takuko

Translations by

Nancy Hamilton

Gabriele Kemesyte

Emily Wan

Katherine Whatley

EXCHANGING CUPS: CONTEMPORARY SAKE POETRY

Dedicated to the memory of Naohiro Goto

後藤直弘氏に捧ぐ

About a year ago, in December 2021, I attended the 蔵開 (*kurabiraki*, a brewery open day), at Hirano Jozo 平野醸造 in Yamato, Gifu Prefecture, in celebration of the new *sake* season. Located in a valley next to the Nagara River, the brewery is celebrating its 150th anniversary in 2023. Though an old tradition harkening back to when *sake* had religious importance and locals only ever drank what was available at their nearby 酒倉 (*sakagura, sake* brewery), the *kurabiraki* had long been forgotten in Yamato until Hirano Jozo revived the event a few years ago. The brewery doors were opened to the community for the weekend and the tiny courtyard was filled with food stalls. When I visited, it had been a year and a half of isolation due to Covid-19—after which, drinking *sake* with others and eating local foods like deer sausage was a welcome comfort. It was also what happened towards the end of the event that was the genesis of this special section of *Mantis*.

To explain, however, I need to rewind some seven hundred years to the fifteenth century. Yamato, located in the Gujo region of Gifu Prefecture in Central Japan, was once an important crossroads between Kyoto and the Kamakura capital, and had a castle run by the Toshi clan. The Toshi are said to have loved poetry, and even stopped a war with a series of poems, or so the local legend says. What we know for sure is that Sogi 宗祗 (1421-1502), the most well-known writer of 連歌 (*renga*, linked poetry from the Medieval era), spent many years there, sponsored by the Toshi clan.

Moving forward a few hundred years, the region became a hotspot for 念仏 (*nenbutsu*, a traditional Buddhist dance). Due to its proximity to the holy mountain, Hakusan, many pilgrims came through the region, bringing with them a new dance culture inflected with religious rites.

Over time the style of dance came to be known as 郡上踊り (*Gujo Odori*) and a version of it continues to be practiced by locals and tourists alike to this day. In fact, the region's dances were registered as a UNESCO Intangible Cultural Heritage in 2023.

A trainee brewer I met that day, Kazuyo Fukao, had moved to the tiny hamlet of Yamato to study *sake* making under Yoshihiro Hioki, the 杜氏 (*toji*, head *sake* maker). Until very recently it was taboo for women to make *sake*, but Fukao was determined to make her own brew after tasting a life-changing wood barrel *sake* brewed in the traditional manner.

Fukao had visited Gujo every August for a number of years, when the region hosts more than thirty days of dancing to honor departed ancestors. It was only once she moved there that she discovered Yamato had been home to Sogi. She started studying *renga* at the local museum focused on poetry history, as well as the celebration songs associated with the dance culture from elders in the region. Working with local rice farmers, she learned that there had once been another song culture that had almost disappeared—work songs that local farmers would sing during the prewar era to make the work go faster and to call on the gods for successful harvests.

Fukao decided to connect this rich song culture with *sake* making. "I wanted to make *sake* that resonated with the land, just like the songs of the region," she reflects. So she worked with local ethnographer, Hiroto Inoue, to seek out elders who still remembered those prewar songs and record them. She folded the songs into the rice making process, teaching them to the volunteers and farmers who came to plant and harvest the *sake* rice. She also worked with Naohiro Goto, a *Gujo odori* singer in his eighties, to create a new celebration song in honor of the new *sake* she created three years ago.

Since becoming the trainee brewer, Fukao has taken on the *kurabiraki*, broadening it from a food and drink event to a community event imbued with poetic history and local culture. *Sake* has long been a topos in East Asian poetry—an age-old inspiration for literati writing late into the night, longing for those far away. Fukao, inspired by both that history and the history of song in Gujo, decided to create a *sake* for drinking while writing poetry. The *sake* is called 一から百 Ichi Kara Hyaku literally translating to "from one to one hundred" and means from start to finish, exemplifying Fukao's focus on taking part on every part of the *sake* process. Visitors at the *kurabiraki* were encouraged to write some tipsy 短歌 (*tanka*) poems (poems with a 5/7/5/7/7 syllabic count, as opposed to *haiku* 俳句 which are 5/7/5) as they enjoyed the new *sake*. The local poetry teacher was on hand to offer assistance and every poet received a hand-calligraphed copy of their poem. Inoue, the local ethnographer, sung the poems aloud in an improvised manner inspired by the more than one thousand year old 朗詠 (*roei*, poetry chanting from the Heian Court). Celebration songs were also sung by Goto and other local singers, folding in a musical culture that had almost been forgotten decades ago.

Along with the festivities at the event, with the assistance of Emi Matsubara, a staff member at the local Kokin Denju Field Museum, Fukao solicited *tanka* about *sake* from poets around Japan. There were close to two hundred submissions from a wide range of poets including: a prisoner, grandparents, schoolteachers, students, office workers. *Mantis* has partnered with Fukao to present a bilingual section of forty-four *tanka* in English and Japanese with translations by Nancy Hamilton, Gabriele Kemesyte, Emily Wan, and me. The poems are about every aspect of *sake*, from production and enjoyment to its cultural context. The breadth speaks to both the importance of *sake* and the *tanka* poetic form in Japanese history and society.

But this project, and the poems themselves, are also about one rural community struggling to survive in the twenty-first century. Because of my interest in traditional Japanese music, I began to visit the Gujo area five years ago. I was moved by the dancing and music which has roots from the sixteenth century, as well as by the locals, transplants and dance fans who are working against odds to make the musical tradition sustainable and the local culture vibrant at a time when Japan is experiencing unprecedented depopulation in rural areas. With cultural products from around the world readily available even in the mountains of Japan, a local brewery might not, at first glance, seem very important. However, Fukao's efforts to reintroduce traditional songs and practices into the *sake* making process shows us that when we lose one community center like a brewery, a whole cultural ecosystem becomes more tenuous, more frayed, and less likely to survive. In contrast, by incorporating previously lost cultural practices like songs, and making the traditions more open and accessible, those cultural events become not mere rote practices everyone has always done, but vital and necessary. Through incorporating poetic and song culture, Fukao and the poets featured here show us that *sake* making in Yamato, in Gujo, in Japan is a vital way of preserving, reinventing and sharing history, tradition and knowledge.

They say that breaking bread and sharing wine is the basis of all culture. I hope that our collection of poems will help connect you to a *sake* culture that means so much to the communities of Yamato, to Fukao, and to me.

Katherine Whatley
December 2022

Forty-four Tanka

translated from Japanese by Nancy Hamilton, Gabriele Kemesyte, Emily Wan, and Katherine Whatley

民宿の炉端で民話聞く初春酒は地酒よ摘みは山菜

listening to tales around the crackling hearth of the local inn
this new year's *sake* is the sake of this place
the snacks, wild shoots gathered from the hills

さだお Sadao

人生の善につけ宴せる日本酒を酌み先ずは乾杯

Celebrating the good things in life
with a round of *sake* –
before all else, "cheers!"

奥山功 Okuyama Isao

ハレの日を祝ふ心のかげりゆくことをとどめよまづは一献

Celebrating a clear day
First, a drink
To stop the heart from darkening

野上卓 Nogami Taku

強面の祖父は俄にほころびぬ「母情」と記さる瓶ひざの上に

my fierce grandfather
suddenly brightens –
Branded with "mother's love"[1]
a *sake* bottle
on his knees

中村佐世子 Nakamura Sayoko

ほんのりと頬を染めたる新成人升酒片手に歓喜の和音

Young adults blushing faintly
fresh wooden *sake* cups held each in one hand
a chorus of delight

大塚美穂 Otsuka Miho

花の下酒ありてこそほのぼのと知らぬ人とも打ちとけあへれ

Under the flowers
It's only because of *sake*
That I warm up a bit
To strangers nearby

恵月 Keigetsu

[1] Mother's love (*bojo* in Japanese) is the main brand of Hirano Jozo Brewing Company. It is
said to be named after the fierce and loving mother of the original founder of the brewery.

浮かれつつさしつさされの花見酒郡上の城に天恵の宴

Making merry
Exchanging cups of
Flower-viewing *sake*
At the castle of Gujo
A banquet of nature's gifts

近藤好廣 Kondo Yoshihiro

満開の桜の下で花見酒一家そろって還暦(かんれき)祝ふ

In full blossom
The sakura; beneath them
Flower-viewing *sake*
One household all gathered for
A sixtieth birthday celebration

原 比呂子 Hara Hiroko

春の桃秋のなでしこうす紅は呑みたき色よ甘い香りす

Peaches of spring
Dianthus flowers of fall
The pale pink is
A color that I want to drink
How sweet the scent it gives

添島貴美代 Soejima Kimiyo

労を田に汗も源米作り一から百酒魂酔うや

Toiling in the paddies
sweat too is
the source of *sake* rice
Brewing from start to finish
my spirit grows tipsy

後藤憲之 Goto Noriyuki

あてもなき一人旅ならローカルを走る車窓に一献捧ぐ

For a solo trip to no place in particular
I take the local train
and raise a glass to the window

阿矢部 僕酔　Ayabe Bokusui

むずかしきことを思わず酌む酒は香り愛しき地元の酒よ

Thinking not of
Difficult things
we pour this *sake*–
And with it
savor the scent of my beloved home

佐藤佐一郎 Sato Saiichiro

亡き父の酔えば歌いし大魚節盆の踊りか遠く聞こゆ

The Obon song that my late father would sing when drinking
I hear it faintly now[2]

旭千代 Asahi Chiyo

この酒は辛口なれどやさしくてこんな上司にわれはなりたし

This *sake* is bold but gentle
I'd like to become
A boss like that

村上秀夫 Murakami Hideo

ビールでも清酒でもよし胸襟を開きて語ることがなによ

Beer or the purest *sake*, both good
for what matters most
loosening the collar and talking heart to heart

野上卓 Nogami Taku

---

2 Obon is the summer festival during which the spirits of ancestors are said to return to
this earth. Though there is Obon dancing throughout Japan, Gujo's Obon dance culture
is unique in that villagers and tourists dance for more than thirty nights compared to the
usual one day a year.

お礼など言えない夫がほろ酔いの口に言えたり言葉すらすら

a husband who cannot utter even a simple thanks
with a little drink
becomes suddenly eloquent

Hayakawa Michiko

露の付くコップ薄目のハイボール夜更の胸を一人洗濯

in this dewy cup
A long highball
A solitary laundering
of my late-night heart

後藤進 Goto Susumu

秋の夜舌にころがす歌がある 一から百酒のすがしき

Autumn night
Rolling on my tongue
A song for *sake*
From beginning to end[3]
A refreshing dryness

田中徹尾 Tanaka Tetsuo

---

3 This poem is referencing the name of the sake, Ichi Kara Hyakushu 一から百酒, meaning the beginning to end sake. But Ichi Kara Hyakushu can also mean the poems from one to one hundred, or the poems that start from beginning to end, as one reading of one character for poem is shu. As such, this poet is making a play on words for this sake and poetry.

季節土地移り変われど変わらぬはああ酒愛し今宵に感謝

Seasons and soil
Though they may move and change
What does not change is—
Ahh, beloved *sake*
Gratitude for this evening

杉本敬治 Sugimoto Keiji

外で飲むこともなくなり一人飲む深夜の酒は望郷ばかり

Going out to drink
Is something I no longer do
I drink alone
This deepening night's *sake*
Is nothing but homesickness

後藤進 Goto Susumu

消しゴムで消せない過去のありまして茶碗の酒が知つております

An eraser
Cannot erase a past
Such as mine
my bowl of *sake*
knows so well

西部 稔 Nishibe Minoru

目が合うは野良猫ばかりそんな日 日本酒の良き香りが喜れし

Only stray cats meet my eyes
On such a day
The nice scent of *sake*
Makes me happy

木村 浩 Kimura Hiroshi

固い物食べにくくなり米すらも磨いて作る日本酒が良し

Hard foods
Become hard to eat
Even rice
But polished into *sake*
It is good

木村浩 Kimura Hiroshi

若き日の君をしのびつつ酔へばなほ恋こふる歌を口ずさぶわれ

Remembering
The days of your youth
I am intoxicated
From my mouth a song
Wishing for you

長畑孝典 Nagahata Takanori

きょうとて明日とて君がいなければ酒すら飲めずどーにかなるよ

Whether today or tomorrow
If you aren't here
I can't even drink
It'll work out somehow

小野木 Onogi

瀬も淵もありて一世の旅路めく長良の川のみなかみの里

Shallow currents and
Deep pools both, like a lifetime's
Journey
The Nagara River
Village at its water's source

村上厚　Murakami Atsushi

よい酒はよい米よい水よい蔵でかもしかもされほろ酔いに

Good *sake*
Is good rice, good water,
And a good brewery
For getting a little stewed in the stewing

Unknown Poet

寒い冬蒸した米達麴かけ杜氏の手指で見事花咲く

Cold winter
Steamed grains of rice
Sprinkling koji[4]
From the chief brewer's fingers
Magnificent blossoms bloom

馬渕貞三 Mabuchi Sadazou

櫂入れてボッコンボッコンかき回す爆発のごと醪は踊る[5]

Insert the paddle
Stir about
Bokkon bokkon
Goes the *sake* mash
Dancing
As if exploding

歌う蔵人 Brewer Poet

---

4 Koji is *Aspergillus oryzae* mold which is used in Japan to make alcoholic beverages like sake, as well as to ferment soybeans to make miso and soy sauce.

5 This poem describes the sounds of the sake after the mash (composed of the already fermented koji and rice starter, yeast, water and steamed rice) have begun to ferment together.

もういいかまだかとのぞきこむ杜氏プツプツ答える樽の中から

is it ready? not quite yet?
the brewer peers inside
the cask grumbles in reply

西口明子 Nishiguchi Akiko

仕込みどき蔵通りゆけばほろ酔いをさそふ香りぞする早暁なりき

During *sake* making season
Wandering past the *sake* brewery
The scent alone invites tipsiness
This early dawn

花田敦子 Hanada Atsuko

真夜中も新酒の仕込み続くらし倉の灯りが冬田を照らす

Even in the dead of night
Making of the new *sake* continues
Continues on
The brewery's lights
Illuminate the winter fields

奥村利夫 Okumura Toshio

くらひらきみなの心もときはなつ体にやどる踊るよろこび

The brewery opens[6]
And the hearts of all
Let loose as well.
Dwelling in the body,
A dancing joy

踊るヴィーガニスタ The Dancing Veganista

東方母情に対し西方のボジレーヌーボ軍配どっち

From the East
Bojo *sake*
From the West
Beaujolais Nouveau
Can one even begin
To compare the two?

吉村卓子 Yoshimura Takuko

「この酒」を「あの酒だ！」という歴史的一瞬がある。その一瞬が好き

This *sake* is that *sake*!
This historic moment
I love that moment

西部稔 Nishibe Minoru

---

6 As mentioned in the editor's notes, this poem is referencing the brewery open day which
though has historical precedence was only recently restarted at Hirano Jozo.

孫十五酒飲めるまであと五年二十は祝うどスナック、屋台

My grandson, fifteen
until he reaches drinking age
another five years
we'll celebrate his twentieth
with bars and food stalls

さだお Sadao

飲むほどにご機嫌になる夫『つま』がいて熱燗『あつかん』おかわり「はいよろこんで」

his mood improving with each drink
he calls for another hot *sake*
"happily!" she replies

木内美由紀 Kiuchi Miyuki

「父ちゃんの命日だね」と空見上げ猪口『ちょこ』で献杯九十『きゅうじゅう』の母

"Today is dad's
death anniversary, isn't it?"
My ninety year old
Mother says
Raising her glass to the sky

木内美由紀 Kiuchi Miyuki

愉しみは余生過ごすに欠かせざる酒のお供に歌学ぶこと

Delight –
together with *sake*,
so irreplaceable
for my remaining days,
learning verses and their ways.

北条暦 Hojo Koyomi

いにしえに思いを馳せて飲む酒は輪廻の水と誰か言ふらむ

The *sake* you drink
When thinking of the past
Is the water of reincarnation
Or so it has been said

凡句楽直 Bonkuranaosu

治療終へ退院来たりて一杯の酒のうまさよ命嘉する

Returning from the hospital
How tasty
This cup of *sake*–
Oh the life I've lived!

星原風堂 Hoshihara Fudo

楽しみは旬の食材調理して肴に夕べ酒を酌む時

Happiness is:
after preparing
seasonal ingredients for
evening appetizers,
the time when we share *sake*

星原風堂 Hoshihara Fudo

澄みわたるこの美酒を育みしは彼方の峰の白雪なるらん

This cloudless
Excellent *sake*–
Who made it so?
Was it the faraway peaks'
White snow?

柾木理花 Masaki Rika

TO RAISE A GLASS, OR DOWN IT: POEMS FOR OUR SPIRITS

Sher Ting Chim
Christopher Honey
Jeff Schiff
Vicky MacDonald Harris
Brandon Marlo
Maggie Bowyer
Nupur Maskara
Gary Bunting
John Peter Beck
David J.S. Pickering
Jenna Cardinale
Mark Schmidt
Will Berry

This one's for the long nights. The ones you think back to—fire warm, snow settling quiet on the sill. Or: refuge from a sudden rain; a chance taken, to enter a door unknown. New haunts, and old. A clean, well-lighted place. A dark corner to hole up in, maybe. Somewhere to just be for a spell.

The knowing smile of someone who knows just what to pour. The flavor of an old companion.

This one's for the worker just getting off the late shift, stopping in for a brew. For the doctor with sore feet, at home at last, swirling a glass of red. For the circle of folks sitting around reminiscing about a friend who isn't there anymore. For the wine and sake makers, for the whiskey distillers. For the one who put down the drink and never picked it back up again. For the bottle gifted after a heartbreak, almost (but not quite) empty. For the sparkling toast to celebrate a union. For the dusty cellar shelves, the forgotten casks, for the angel's share. For sunlight held together by water, for harmonies of nature's blessings and human wisdom.

It's something we share, a flow of culture that runs through us—something we share, too, with the muses and gods. Some might call it poetry distilled. Some might say poetry wouldn't exist without it (they'd be wrong—poetry is, of course, always). But still, delights unfolding—a pucker of the lips, tickle of the fancy, turn of the phrase, lilt of the line, just one more glass, perhaps, of—

Hours well spent, after all is said, and the sounds fade and give way to thought, to reverie, to wonder. How lucky we are, to be left with notes to linger on, something to ruminate on before we go. How lucky we are to share moments, to have these words that reside in the space between us, bridging, flowing, offering us another chance to indulge.

Invocation:

Pour one out for time lost, and for all the people along the way.
And raise a glass for remembrance. For them, and you.

Jason Beckman
April 2023

Sher Ting Chim

Whoever Says Everything Gets Better With Age Has Never Drunk Snake Wine

O,
The burden of sobriety.

旧and 酒: Why do we drink
except to forget about the past?

My grandfather once
bit into
tapioca and cried.

My grandfather once screamed
at the sound of a car backfiring
into the abyss.

How does it feel to be lost
to time?

My grandfather sometimes forgets
and shouts at the Mazdas passing
on the streets.

My grandfather still calls it
shinbun, instead of
新闻.

My grandfather still sleeps next to
a gun, in the echo from the hills,
in which he fought sticks

Against
better judgment.

Was it anxiety
or nostalgia
that kept him awake?

The bullet leaves
the bones of the soldiers
of the 42nd battalion —

Through the white
winter halls
of the Municipal Building,

Through bloodied and marred
surrender documents, dotted
and signed,

Through the General that has
returned to
an orphaned crowd,

Desperate to reclaim
what he has
abandoned.

It lodges in Ah Gong's solar
plexus, rattling in the
bones of a clock.

Learning the
hum of changing skies,

Dawn coloured
the whistle of wine,

My grandfather wakes at
6am and stares out at the
erupted vegetable field

Until he remembers
this day has been won.

A drink is still a drink until it
falls off the table at both ends.

What is time
but a soldier leaning

Into another
trust-fall

In the arms

Of a larger
gravity.

Christopher Honey
A Dirty, Badly Lit Place

A green glass whisky bottle sits himself
Across from me, looks over the table of
Matched water ring stains, accrued over wasted years
He could have spent on travel, making love
To champagne flutes and brandy snifters, broad
Hungry and rich. "My life's been built on dumb
Mistakes," he sighs. – "A glass," he suddenly
Demands aloud. "Please," he adds. "One pour more,"
He tells me, "Just the one tonight, that's all."
        He says, "Oblige me, sir. Let's smoke cigarettes
And drink all night, as if we were old friends.
Friends with bad history, but who still have chosen
To forget old betrayals, lovers lost,
And anything that interferes with good
Drink, conversation, or the making of
New memories to keep us warm tomorrow."
        We drink all night – life's coin is spent and spilled
Until I say farewell to my empty
Friend to bid sunny morning my hellos.

Jeff Schiff
They'll drunk

or sun-lulled or too too
       to give a good goddamn
              leave their flotsam

bobbing
       or snagged on windfall branches
              where the draft is too shallow

for eco-conscience to prevail
       or where snappers are rumored
              and one dare not toe in

stuff chucked in vengeance
       stuff that's knocked or slips over gunwale
              or off deck rails

commemorative hats family reunion kit
       orphaned sandals
              dead soldier empties

Chardonnay bottles that'll one day wash up
       messaging no one
              with nothing to say

Vicky MacDonald Harris
The Whisky Had Other Plans

In the old world where you
tromped freely around the mountain
Highlands, where geology housed our branch
of the clan, the small primrose
and thistle tacked west. Now riven,
the fiddles and violins carve
the song of the new, spin wood
into notes, and bows into perfect
dry strung fifths.

Brandon Marlo

zero

Five little words in my head.
"Should I really hit send"
I hit send.
Four dollars left after rent.
A few more on the lend.
I let my pride bend.
(Just a little)
Three more questions: A Thread
Am I well groomed? Well fed?
I guess I'm not dead?
Then it's Two glasses of Italian red.
Sushi and a hit from the weed pen.
A late night visit from a friend.
One last tango in my bed.
At least that's what I said
To myself.
Don't tell her I told you.

Maggie Bowyer

A Rough Draft of the Drunk Text I am Typing From the Bar Bathroom

Hey I know it's been a while and our whole past is checkered, but this isn't about that / I am at the bar / which probably sounds normal for me but in truth / I haven't drank in two and a half years / yet now I'm here / I met a girl with wild curly hair and she told me she has pain beyond repair / tells me she lays in bed catatonic for four days a month / tells me there are knives on her insides that breathe fire when she tosses one back / precisely why she's drinking a mocktail / I told her about the demons growing inside us / insidious and taboo / burrowing into our tissue / I pounded three more shots / I warned you I am a lightweight now / your face replaced hers / her hair straighter and her face full of freckles / my brain filled to the brim with once compressed memories / your doctor performs ablation / charring your insides and doing nothing but enraging deep disease / she gives out pills like they are candy rather than poison / you deserve to have competent surgery / I am writing this message to add some key sources to your research / I am writing because I feel as guilty as your doctor / I am writing because even if I hate you / you don't deserve your insides to be whittled down and then burned / I am writing because I am sorry / I am writing because I was wrong / I am writing because I am afraid and angry / I am writing because the guilt feels almost as damning as this disease / I am writing / I am erasing / I am sorry

Nupur Maskara
It's the Wine Talking

I slosh around in his glass,
He swirls me around in his mouth.
Ugh.
I hate meeting his saliva.

The stories he tells?
I get the real dope,
When I circulate in his blood.
His cells are chatty,

Glad to have a visitor.
I tell them I'm from France.
They've never been anywhere,
They don't know I grew in India.

"He's a philanderer," says Lil' Billy
"I don't get any rest. You make it
Easier for him to get action," he glares.
I feel myself redden more, if that's possible.

"His thoughts alone could jail him," sighs his one brain cell.
"I'm tired of the eating, smoking, talking," moans his jaw.
"I've got to digest that," says his stomach acidly.
"I have to work double when you're around," they chorus.

Like a firefly, I live a night.
A night to remember for him. Or
One that he'd rather not remember.
Heh heh.

Gary Bunting
Fuzzy Outtakes

I don't really drink
I don't really know what kind of drunk I am
But yesterday I got slightly tipsy
Slightly squiffy on red wine
Turns out I'm an introspective drunk who
Cries at Whitney Houston songs
I mean, those notes, y'know?

I found myself hypnotized
My eyes drawn to the brake lights
Burning on the cars ahead of us
Have you ever seen the Manhattan skyline at midnight?
When your wide eyes are drawn to every single light
Their reflections quivering in the East river
The Brooklyn Bridge like a Chinese dragon
Fire breathing across the glittering black, sparkling black water.

My legs felt like Velcro unhooking
My head like popped bubble wrap.
I wrote a haiku
In my head but now it's gone
The greatest haiku?
I guess we'll never know
But I'll guess not.

Oh these fuzzy outtakes
Water tower mosaic images
Neon cakes and wires shaking
Seating, standing

Standing seating
Bacon sandwiches, pop tambourines beating
A thimbleful of sleep in the passenger seat
I laugh at a sign as we pass a garage closed for the night
It says 'Lube Entrance' in pink neon lights

John Peter Beck
Pinochle Poem #1

This morning,
I feel like I have been
lying at the bottom

of a gallon of cheap red wine,
but all I had was just one beer.

It must have been
the cards.

It must be
a pinochle hangover
from having
too many lousy hands.

Well, I'm paying
for that card game now.

Nothing to do
but take an aspirin
or stay in bed,

and I'm out of both.

David J.S. Pickering

Pain Has No Memory in Rockaway Beach Oregon

Luke 4:24

No prophet is welcome in his hometown,
and come next summer locals will forget
forewarnings of clouds, omens of breakdown.
No prophet is welcome. In this hometown
divorcees smoke all day in old nightgowns,
exes drunk by noon slurring epithets.
No prophet is welcome in his hometown,
and come next summer locals will forget.

Jenna Cardinale

Two Dreams

After our boat sinks, we sit
on the side not touching
the ocean floor. We can breathe
without effort, so we stay here
and watch the whales
play above.

Jam jars filled
with cocktails for
consumption by
the constant lake.
We have popsicles after,
in our own apartments.

Mark Schmidt
Anticlimax

Human-sized constellation
So prickly like a slept limb
　　　Or lumps of regret
　　　Wine-flavored
Caught in the teeth of trees
The moon the clouds we
Irrigate our beds nightly–

Lack of always, we buffer
The sideways and cluttered
Mind of wine so full of holes
And car departingly whining–
"Why, why I" says the
Infinity in your back pocket–
　　　You stay sitting.

But cords bind our minds
Cords sown in the vineyard
So wetted with wisdomless words with
　　　Day-old makeup
　　　Paint flaking
The reflection of a mirror
More profound than a single sunset
More than god's last breath
Bottled and sold at a flea market–
Thy will be scorned on earth as it is
　　　In hell.

Why core the apple and riposte–
Arsenic lips you have my dear–
Why approach with the gait of
A chair or a wobbling table–
　　　　Back off vile thing
　　　　Thou hyena thou
Bandit– who sold you the map leading
　　　　To me?
Who is the unlucky one to befriend me
In such a slum as my mind?

Will Berry
"Jacob, Jacob."

In the yellow house my mother stopped calling me by name.
A mere infant, I'd whine and spit up on her shirt. She didn't mind.
She'd swaddle me in flannel and hum maritime lullabies as hammers
    clanged around us.
My father yanked up floorboards. His crew chipped away plaster.
By end of summer, the house would sit afresh.
But something in the framework awoke.
Mornings, men would find nails pulled out,
varnish scratched, tools askew atop ladders.
My mother later told me how they'd look over their shoulders,
afraid of something they couldn't put their calloused hands on.
Something lurking like arsenic in faded wallpaper.
One contractor rigged a camcorder in the attic, a "ghost trap" he called it.
Next morning, he checked his camera, walked out, and never came back.

It's our first apartment together.
My girlfriend tells me there's a friendly ghost.
One that misplaces glasses of orange juice.
One that waters our hanging plants.
One that re-folds the dish towels.
"Isn't that nice, Jay?" she says as if our tawny cat
learned to waddle on his haunches and vacuum his own hairballs.
She invites her friend who reads tarot to examine our rooms.
I hold our cat, who squirms at the girl's omnipresent scent of sage and weed.
After pacing our hallway, the tarot girl concludes there's indubitably a
    presence.
"No wonder." She side-eyes me and says,
"This one dragged him in."

Age six, I took to the fields outside my grandfather's farmhouse,
seeking friends among foundation stones, unearthing cicadas.
"Jake Jr., don't roam too far."
My mother sipped coffee across from my grandfather — my father's father.
Perhaps he once had the posture of his son, but even hunched over,
his shadow loomed large against the doorframe.
The abandoned chicken barn was filled with cans again.
My father once took me along to the redemption center, made forty-
    seven bucks.
He let me hold the bills in my hand.
By the road, the neighbor's kid threw stones at peeling birches.
We swapped ghost stories.
He said his older sister saw
a little girl playing in the halls of the Tideside Tavern.
I had it on good authority from my babysitter
that circus clowns tiptoe along the train tracks.
He said never look up at West End widow's walks.
Veiled faces will stare back.
I told him my cousin said to never piss behind the Clam Shack.
An old lobsterman will trap your soul in his nets.
He said the worst of all is down Summer Street
in the yellow house.
A haunting so horrible,
no one dares speak its name.
I mentioned my father worked on the renovations.
The kid then claimed he heard his mom call and ran off.
I returned to the farmhouse porch. My grandfather was laughing.
He said my father never had to fire anyone — they all quit.
My mother only smiled.

Years later, I'm driving down Summer Street.
Red lights illuminate the fog.
Paramedics hoist a gurney into the yellow house.
The lady there fell, broke her neck.
"Old house, steep stairs," a store clerk tells me.

"The people change, but that place stays the same."

In the mirror, you could accuse me of dating my mother;
but live with my girlfriend, you'll see I'm dating my father.
She shares his taste in decor of empty bottles.
Hers, on display above cabinets, a habit from her college years.
His, hidden in closets, between linens, gathering dust under cupboards.
Upon moving in together, we agreed she could only keep one.
She stuffed a musty fifth of Jack with burnt-out fairy lights
and left it by the windowsill.
It's the only thing our cat hasn't knocked over,
so it sits there.
Some nights, when I come home late from the lumberyard,
when I'm alone in the kitchen,
I can see the bottle glow.
"Jay, come to bed now."
None of my names feel like my own.
They're just noises I wake up to.
My grandfather told me there's a mass grave in his backyard.
A fox in the barn caused the chickens to panic,
throw themselves against walls,
claw at each other.
He and my father buried them behind the farmhouse.
It was time my dad learned to use the backhoe.
He was six.

By end of renovations, the new owners from Boston worried.
They had heard the stories.
Thus hired a medium to perform a cleansing.
The Bostonians and their acquaintances put down their merlot
and held hands as the medium whisked sage
throughout every chamber,
all the way to the attic.
The houseguests giggled
as their cocktails tickled them.

But a hush crept over the party
as the medium's footsteps creaked
back down
each step.
She said,
"There's a presence.
He's up in the linen cupboard.
His name is Jacob."

My girlfriend has a vision for our apartment.
She plans to revarnish the floorboards,
chip away plaster,
revive the antique wallpaper.
She's asked me to bring back tools from work.
I apologize because I keep forgetting.
But I don't.

I was playing by the barn when my mother threw me in the back seat.
I was confused because my father said we'd all eat lunch together.
"He can't make it," my mother said.
We drove away. Away from the farmhouse.
Between fields. Past graveyards.
Beyond the yellow house.
It would be years before I saw that place again.

"The dirt is yours," the executor tells me.
I'm on the phone while my girlfriend grooms our cat.
Hairs on the doormat.
Hairs on the duvet.Hairs on our hand towels.
That cat will sleep anywhere,
except the linen closet.

I find myself walking across fields.
My father stands there,
offers me promised land.

A wall of trees define its borders.
I step towards the edge.
There, I see yellow slats between birches.
Go on, he says, take a look.

A thump from the linen closet.
My girlfriend nudges me awake.
"Jacob, Jacob."

TRANSLATIONS

Kumar Pranjal Rai
Carolina Esses
Okura of Yama-no-Ue
George Sarantaris
Rolf Gjedsted
Muyaka bin Haji al-Ghassaniy
Murilo Mendes
Mihai Eminescu
Gad Kaynar-Kissinger
Yan Rong
Ezequiel Naya

Kumar Pranjal Rai
नदी, स्वप्न और तुम्हारा पता

मैं जग रहा हूँ
आँखों में गाढ़ी चिपचिपी थकान भरे
कि नींद मेरे विकल्पों की सूची में खो गयी है कहीं।
जिस बिस्तर पर मैं लेटा
चाहे-अनचाहे मेरी उपस्थिति का गवाह बनकर छूट गयी कुछ सलवटें
छूटी हुई उन सलवटों में निवेश था मेरे अस्तित्व का।
वह बीते दिनों की बात है
जब मैं स्वप्न में तुमसे मिलने आता था,
तुम अक्सर नदी किनारे एक छोटा सा घर बनाने का ख़्वाब बुनती थीं।
जब आख़िरी बार मिले थे वहाँ
तो तुम्हारे पाँवों में चोट थी
तुम्हारे रक्त की बूँदें मेरे स्वप्न पर गिरी थीं,
अगले रोज जब मलहम लेकर आया
तो तुम नहीं मिली थीं उस पते पर।
एक सरहद आकर लेट गयी थी तकियों के बीच
लेकिन सरहदों को मैंने नींद की चादर नहीं बनने दिया।
और विकल्पों की सूची से
नींद के विदा हो जाने पर भी
व्यक्ति अपने सपनों से विद्रोह नहीं कर सकता।
अब मैं खुली आँखों में बुनता हूँ स्वप्न,
मैं चेतना की नाव पर सवार चलता हूँ
अक्षरों को पत्तों पर सँभालकर विसर्जित करता हूँ नदी में,
पत्ता काँपता है नदी की साँस पर

translated from Hindi by Pitamber Kaushik
The River, Dreams, and Your Whereabouts

I stay awake,
eyes filled with viscous, glutinous weariness
for sleep has since been lost in my long list of alternatives.

The bed that I lay upon,
notwithstanding my volition, has registered a few creases and wrinkles
testifying to my presence;
My existence is invested in those leftover wrinkles and folds.

It's a matter of days long past
when I used to visit you in dreams.
You would oftentimes weave an aspiration
to build a dainty riverside cottage.
When we last met there
your feet were bruised
Your blood had dripped on my dreams;
When I returned with salve the next day,
you were not to be found there.

A frontier had since lain itself down between the pillows
But I never let frontiers serve as the sheets of slumber –
even following the departure of sleep
from one's list of alternatives
can a man dare not rise in rebellion against his dreams.

Nowadays, I weave dreams with open eyes,
I ride the boat of consciousness
conveying my homage by means of leaves carefully-lain with letters set
    adrift,

और तलाशता है तुम्हारा पता
कि नींद के बाहर किस किनारे पर घर है तुम्हारा,
कहाँ मिलोगी अब तुम, खुली आँखों के स्वप्न में!

the leaf trembles in the breath of the river
as it seeks your whereabouts
as to on what banks beyond slumber stands your house,
where are you to be found, in the dreams of eyes wide open!

Carolina Esses
Amiga, nunca tuve buena memoria

pero ahora apenas recuerdo
la idea del viaje.
Deberíamos haber previsto
esta inconsistencia de la voluntad
este desgano. Hubiese sido necesario
un documento escrito, algo más
que tu voz ensayada para recorrer distancias.

Intento recordar, no creas que no lo hago
pero apenas repito alguna de nuestras palabras
ella cae a mis pies, como una piedra.
Desde aquí solo puedo ver un pino, una liebre,
un refugio apenas habitable. Y no es el mío.

Entonces me escondo en el invernadero.
Soy una planta más enredada entre sus propias raíces
y espero a que ella, jardinera hábil y paciente,
se incline sobre mis hojas
como sobre su propio alimento.
Si vinieras, me encontrarías
en el hueco de su mano.

translated from Spanish by Allison deFreese

My memory was never any good, my friend

but now I can barely remember
the reason for this trip.
We should have foreseen
our inconsistent motivation,
this lack of enthusiasm. We should have
put something in writing, had something more
than your measured voice to span distance.

I'm trying to remember, don't think I'm not,
but I've barely repeated any of our words
that fall like stones at my feet.
From here, I only see a pine tree, a hare,
a barely habitable shelter. A refuge not my own.

So I hide in the greenhouse
just another plant tangled in my own roots
waiting for her, for the graceful, patient gardener
to lean over my leaves
and nourish herself.
If you appeared now, you would find me
cupped in the palm of her hand.

Amiga, ¿dónde quedaba mi casa?

¿y de qué lado de la calle debíamos encontrarnos?
El ómnibus que me lleva de vuelta
va paralelo a un bosque
luego veo un descampado.
La mayor parte del viaje sueño con un tren
que lleva mujeres vestidas de verde. Yo voy de rojo,
tengo un hijo que envuelvo entre mi saco
pero desaparece cuando despierto.
¿Serías mi hijo? ¿Podría acunarte
como me acunaba el bosque?

Where does my house sit, my friend?

and on what side of the street shall we meet?
The bus that takes me back follows the edge of the forest,
then I see an open field.
For most of the trip, I dream of a train
that carries women dressed in green. I'm in red,
a child wrapped in my jacket,
but he disappears when I awaken.
Will you be my son? Can I rock you to sleep
like the forest rocks me to sleep?

Okura of Yama-no-Ue

男子名は古日に恋ひたる歌三首　長一首短二首
山上憶良

世の人の　貴び願ふ　七種の　宝も我れは　何せむに　わが中の
　生れ出でたる　白玉の　我が子古日は　明星の　明くる朝は
敷栲の　床の辺去らず　立てれども　居れども　共に戯れ　夕星
の　夕になれば　いざ寝よと　手をたづさはり　父母も　うへはな
さかり　さきくさの　中にを寝むと　愛しく　しが語らへば　いつ
しかも　人と成り出でて　あしけくも　よけくも見むと　大船の　思
ひ頼むに　思はぬに　横しま風の　にふふかに　覆ひ来れば　為
むすべの　たどきを知らに　白栲の　たすきを懸け　真澄鏡　手
に取り持ちて　天つ神　仰ぎ乞ひ禱み　国つ神　伏して額つき
かからずも　かかりも　神のまにまにと　立ちあざり　我れ乞ひ禱
めど　しましくも　よけくはなしに　やくやくに　かたちくづほり　朝
な朝な　言ふことやみ　たまきはる　命絶えぬれ　立ち躍り　足す
り叫び　伏し仰ぎ　胸打ち嘆き　手に持てる　我が子飛ばしつ
世間の道

反歌
若ければ　道行き知らじ　賄はせむ　黄泉の使　負ひて通らせ
布施置きて　我れは祈ひ禱む　あざむかず　直に率行きて　天道
知らしめ

Note: Chinese characters have been replaced or complemented by kana for readability.

translated from Classical Japanese by Seiji Hakui

A Song to Miss a Boy Named Furuhi, followed by two Envois

The seven treasures[*1] people praise
And hope to own to me
Were nothing, for to us was born
Our white pearl, Furuhi.

At daybreak where the morning star
Would proclaim a new day,
He would not leave our bed so he
With us could longer play.

At dusk the evening star would shine;
Would he to our hands cling
And ask, "I want you by my side
While I am sound sleeping.

So, mom, dad, please let us lie down
Together side by side."
Such a lovely thing to say. He was
Truly our joy and pride.

We anticipated seeing him,
Should he be good or bad,
Grow up into a man. Was such
The hope in him we had.

But all at once a baleful wind
O'er him did sideways blow.
What means we had to save his life,
Did not at all I know.

I therefore on my shoulder wore
A sash of snow white cloth
And took up my clearest mirror[2]
To beg those great gods both:

I prayed unto the gods above[3],
Eyes fixed at their blue sky;
To pray unto the gods of earth[4],
I down in dirt did lie.

Upset and vexed I prayed so that
The gods' will might alone
Decide my child should live or die:
My prayers did I intone.

But not for a moment he got well:
My child's complexion got
More pallid day by day; with me
Now he could chatter not.

His life ended, so I sprang up
And stamped, crying, my feet.
And I fell down, and I gazed up;
With grief my chest I beat.

I had had him right in my arms
But I let him be hurled[5] –
My dear child was taken from me.
O, the way of the world!

The Envois:

O, guide of Yomi*⁶,
Please carry him on your back, I shall pay
The toll: the young child would not know the way.

Leaving the toll here,
I pray you not to lead my child astray,
But please lead him to heaven straightaway.

Translator's Notes

1. The seven treasures: gold, silver, lapis lazuli, crystals, shells of the giant clam, corals, and agate. The concept originated in the Sukhāvatīvyūha Sūtra.
2. My clearest mirror: A round bronze mirror. Round mirrors have been regarded as symbols of the sun goddess in Shinto since Amaterasu bid her grandson Ninigi to enshrine the sacred mirror Yata-no-Kagami in her remembrance.
3. The gods above: The gods of heaven. The top of the hierarchy is Amaterasu.
4. The gods of earth: The gods that belong to earth. The top of the hierarchy is O-Ana-Muchi, the son of Susanoo (the younger brother of Amaterasu and the moon god Tsukuyomi) and Princess Kushinada (a goddess of earth whom Susanoo saved from the eight-headed dragon Yamata no Orochi).
5. I let him be hurled: Some scholars take this line literally, that is to say the speaker, who is bawling, falling down and jumping up with the dead child in his arms, accidentally flings the corpse away. But here I followed the figurative interpretation: what the speaker means is that he failed to save his child.
6. Yomi: The land of the dead in Japanese mythology. The creator goddess Izanami became the ruler of Yomi after she gave birth to the fire god Kagutsuchi and died of burn injuries.

George Sarantaris

Ἀγαπάω τὸν ὕπνο
γιατὶ κι αὐτὸς ἀγαπάει τὴν ψυχή μου,
καὶ μοῦ σκεπάζει τὰ μάτια
μὲ τὰ λουλούδια ποὺ θέλω.

Βαίνω πρὸς τὴ θάλασσα
Μὰ κυττάω τ' ἀστέρια
Βάρος στὸν καθρέφτη
Ὅπου ὁ πόθος μου
Μαρμαρυγὴ ἀπὸ τὰ ρίγη τοῦ νεροῦ

Τούτη ἡ φωνὴ εἶναι βαθειὰ σὰ λουλούδι

Μὴν τὴν μολύνεις· θὰ σοῦ πεῖ τὸ πρόσωπό σου
Ὅταν ἀστράφτει πάνω ἀπ' τοὺς γύρους τοῦ καιροῦ
...
Μὴν πετάξεις προτοῦ ἡ δίψα σου γράψει τὸ οὐράνιο τόξο
Καὶ οἱ πετεινοὶ ἐπαινέσουν τ' ὄνομά σου

I love sleep
because it loves my soul in turn
and covers my eyes
with the flowers of my choice

I head for the sea
But I watch the stars
Burden on the mirror
Where my desire
Glimmers from the tremors of water

This voice is deep like a flower

Don't taint it—it will reveal your face
When it shines above the circuit of time
...
Don't fly off until your thirst scribes the rainbow
And the roosters laud your name

Rolf Gjedsted
For ikke at brænde

For ikke at brænde,
gør jeg mig ét med ilden.
For ikke at drunkne,
forener jeg mig med vandet.
For ikke for ofte at forstille mig,
forestiller jeg mig,
at alt inden i,
foregår som alt uden for,
med visse modifikationer.

Der er tale om en balance
mellem salte og vædsker,
temperatur og natur,
noget mere end en ren kemi.

Når vi er sammen,
åbner vi hver gang
døren for en uafsøgt mulighed
uden for og inden i os selv,
til et stumt liv,
der venter på at få en stemme.

translated from Danish by Michael Favala Goldman
To Keep from Burning Up

To keep from burning up
I make myself one with fire.
To keep from drowning,
I unite with water.
To not isolate myself too often,
I imagine
that everything inside me
transpires like everything on the outside
with certain modifications.

This includes a balance
between salts and fluids,
temperature and nature,
more than simply chemistry.

When we are together,
each time we open
the door to a chance possibility
outside of and within ourselves,
for a mute life
waiting to gain a voice.

Muyaka bin Haji al-Ghassaniy
Natamani Vuta Nyanje

Natamani vuta nyanje ila k'ambaa ni mbovu
Tumo kubadili ngwenje kununua zenyi nguvu:
Na wale wenyi vipanje si wajinga ni welevu,
Watutenda wapumbavu tungawa nazo kitwani.

translated from Swahili by Richard Prins
I Wish

I wish I could be trendy, but all my threads are tattered.
Look at us counting pennies for something finely tailored.
The ones with all the money just keep on getting smarter.
They make us look like suckers, for all the brains in our head.

Ufukara Enda Zako

Ufukara enda zako mimi nawe tuwegene
Silitaki shari lako kawatafute wengine
Uwatie pujuliko mitima iwasonone
Uniwene nikuwene, salama salimini!

Destitution Get Thee Gone

Destitution, get thee gone. You and me, we're over.
I don't want your misfortune. Find someone else to bother.
Let them have your confusion; now their spirit can suffer.
And if we see each other, say hello, then go in peace.

Ai, Ulimwengu Jivu

Ai, ulimwengu jivu, ujileo vumbivumbi,
Walifile waangavu wali na wao ujimbi,
Vianga havia mbivu viwiti vya ufurumbi;
Wale walimbika k'ambi leo ndio walimbikwa.

Ndiyo, hali ya dunia, huleta vyema na vimbi,
Ambaye yamtatia maninga yakwe hafumbi;
Usingizi hupotea kwa mawazo t'umbit'umbi.
Wale walimbika k'ambi leo ndio walimbikwa

The World Is Ash

The world is nothing but ashes, and it is getting dusty.
They died while shining brightest, although they were so cocky.
The young fruit gets no ripeness; the green leaf gets so stinky.
They used to call the assembly. Now they're the ones who are called.

That's just the way of the world, bringing us good and bad things.
Whoever it has embroiled must keep their eyes from closing.
Every chance at sleep is spoiled by their constant worrying.
They used to call the gathering. Now they're the ones who are called.

Murilo Mendes
O Homem e a Água

As mãos têm hélice, tempestade e bússola.
Os pés guardam navios
Aparelham para o Oriente
O olho tem peixes,
A boca, recifes de coral;
Os ouvidos têm noites polos e lamento de ondas.

A vida é muito marítima.

translated from Portuguese by Baz Martin Gibbons
Man and Water

Hands of propellers, storm and compass.
Feet keep ships
Shipshape for the East
The eye has fish,
The mouth its coral reefs;
Ears of nights, poles, and wailing waves.

Life is exceedingly maritime.

A Liberdade

Um buquê de nuvens:

O braço duma constelação
Surge entre as rendas do céu.

O espaço transforma-se a meu gosto,
É um navio, uma ópera, uma usina,
Ou então a remota Persépolis.

Admiro a ordem da anarquia eterna,
A nobreza dos elementos
E a grande castidade da Poesia.

Dormir no mar! Dormir nas galeras antigas!

Sem o grito dos náufragos,
Sem os mortos pelos submarinos.

Liberty

A bouquet of clouds:

The arm of a constellation
pops up among heavenly lace.

Space transforms to my whim,
it's a ship, an opera, a power plant,
or far off Persepolis.

I admire the order of eternal anarchy,
the nobility of the elements
and the grand chastity of Poetry.

To sleep at sea! To sleep in ancient galleys!

Without the cry of castaways,
without those drowned by submarines.

Mihai Eminescu
Odă

(în metru antic)

Nu credeam să-nvăț a muri vrodată;
Pururi tânăr, înfășurat în manta-mi,
Ochii mei nălțam visător la steaua
                                    Singurătății.

Când deodată tu răsăriși în cale-mi,
Suferință tu, dureros de dulce...
Pân-în fund băui voluptatea morții
                                    Nendurătoare.

Jalnic ard de viu chinuit ca Nessus,
Ori ca Hercul înveninat de haina-i;
Focul meu a-l stinge nu pot cu toate
                                    Apele mării.

De-al meu propriu vis, mistuit mă vaiet,
Pe-al meu propriu rug, mă topesc în flacări...
Pot să mai renviu luminos din el ca
                                    Pasărea Phoenix?

Piară-mi ochii turburători din cale,
Vino iar în sân, nepăsare tristă;
Ca să pot muri liniștit, pe mine
                                    Mie redă-mă!

translated from Romanian by Delia Radu
Ode

(in Sapphic stanzas)

Never did I contemplate learning death's game
Young forever I believed I'd be, proudly
Wore my mantle, dreamily worshipped the fierce
        Star of aloneness.

All at once you, suffering, crossed my pathway,
Out you stood, voluptuous; your seductive
Magic brew, so painfully sweet, I drank down;
        Death-like it tasted.

Now I'm broken, tortured like Nessus, aching,
Or like poisoned Hercules in the centaur's
Blood smeared shirt; extinguish this fire no one can,
        Even the sea can't.

Moaning, as my own dream devours me, sobbing,
Melting down in flames, at my own stake burning...
Will I ever rise from the ashes shining
        Bright like a phoenix?

Troubling eyes, from me go away, depart now
Come to me, indifference, constant, sad friend,
So I die in peace, you return myself to
        Me, let me find me!

Gad Kaynar-Kissinger

גד קינר-קיסינגר

על הראיה

Truly, it is in the darkness that one finds the light, so when we are in sorrow, then this light is nearest of all to us.

(Meister Eckhart)

לשלמה בידרמן

אֵין דָּבָר הַמַּכְבִּיד עַל הָרְאִיָּה מִן הָאוֹר.
הַשֶּׁמֶשׁ מַשְׁטִיחָה וּמַשְׁחִיתָה אֶת הַכֹּל לְאֶחָד.
מֶרְכַּבְתּוֹ שֶׁל הֶלְיוֹס, בִּינָתוֹ שֶׁל אַפּוֹלּוֹן,
הֵן תַּעְתּוּעַ.
רַק בַּצֵּל, בָּאַפְלוּלִית, רַק בִּשְׁעַת אֵבֶל,
כְּשֶׁהָאוֹר נֶאֱבָק עִם הַשָּׁחוֹר,
אֲנַחְנוּ רוֹאִים אֶת הַחַיִּים.
אַחֲרֵי שֶׁמֵּתוּ.
No news, good news.
אִמִּי הָיְתָה אוֹמֶרֶת:

כְּשֶׁאֵשֶׁת לוֹט הָפְכָה לִנְצִיב מֶלַח
הִיא גִּלְּתָה אֶת הָאֹשֶׁר הָאֲמִתִּי.
הָאֵשׁ בִּסְדוֹם דָּעֲכָה
רַק שׁוּעָלִים וְתַנִּים חִפְּשׂוּ פְּגָרִים
בֵּין הַהֲרִיסוֹת.
מַבָּטָהּ קָבַע בָּרִיק עַד עוֹלָם.
דָּבָר לֹא יָכוֹל הָיָה לְהַפְתִּיעָהּ.
דָּבָר לֹא יָכוֹל הָיָה לִפְגֹּעַ בָּהּ.
אִישׁ לֹא חָשַׁק בְּגוּף הַמֶּלַח שֶׁלָּהּ.
הִיא יָדְעָה מַשֶּׁהוּ שֶׁאִישׁ לֹא יָדַע.
מֵתָה חַיָּה.
אֵין אֹשֶׁר גָּדוֹל מִזֶּה.

translated from Hebrew by Natalie Fainstein
On Sight

To Shlomo Biderman

Nothing Burdens the sight more than light.
The sun defiles and flattens all into one.
Helios' chariot, Apollo's wisdom
Are but an illusion.
Only in shadow, in shade, or in mourning
As the light battles darkness,
Do we see the living.
After they died.

My mother used to say:
No news, good news.
When Lot's wife turned into a pillar of salt
She discovered true happiness.
The fire in Sodom died down
Foxes and jackals alone looked for carcasses
In the ashes.
Her gaze fixated in the void for eternity.
Nothing could surprise her.
Nothing could harm her.
No one lusted after her salty flesh.
She knew something no one else did.
She, alive and dead.
There's no greater joy.

Yan Rong
梅花引 · 白鸥问我泊孤舟

为什么要问，都是岸，都是舟
都是鸟。我会留下我所有的器官
他们还想复制我十年的想法
这不太可能，我愿意但
他们不太可能。即使我皱眉
生病，他们也会犯下乐观之错
我捂着胸口，他们跳起幼儿园的舞

寒风最可爱，小窗口可爱
灯以及它发出的光也可爱
寂寞也可爱，寂寞的身体尤其可爱
我像纸一样被撕开，我看见
他们一张张被慢慢撕开——作为纸
这之前我往里面添了好多星期
好多中年的低沉之音，好多嘶哑

这桌面是旧游，它像田野
这杯子是旧游，它像扎向白天的根
而绝不再有黑夜。我把一个国家
都搬进来了，让他们尽管
开会并举手，让他们打开电视看新闻
讨论第二天要进的货，哦或者
未来的照片，在任何可以绽放的地方

梦最可爱，梦不到最最可爱
在梦里我赞美寒水空流，我赞美白雪
我赞美一场大雨湿透我的衣服
我赞美无人愁似我，我赞美他们拿着碗

我赞美他们为我做着安检
我赞美雪有这么大，梅花这么小
我赞美我的晚餐，为能藏起一根肋骨

translated from Chinese by Ravi Shankar

Plum Blossoms · White Gull Asks After my Lonely Boat

Why ask any more questions? The answer's all shore,
all boats, all birds. I will leave behind my organs for science.
They still want to replicate my thoughts posthumously.
This is improbable. I am willing but believe it quite unlikely.
Even if I pinch my eyebrows and cough up blood, they would
still tell me a cheery fable of optimism and call it facts.
I could be doubled over while they dance a kindergarten dance.

Cold wind's the cutest, the window, the solitary bulb, the light
it casts cute as well. Loneliness is also cute, its isolated body
particularly so. I'm shredded like paper with each passing day.
Just this week, I added a lot of middle-aged gripes to my husk.

This tabletop is an old trip like the fields where hardwood grew.
This cup is also an old trip, a root branching into daytime,
neglecting the dark nights when it got repurposed. I have moved here
an entire country. Let them host town halls and raise their hands.
Let them turn on the TV to watch new news and then congregate
to discuss tomorrow's imports, to sketch pictures from the future,
and to build fertile human spaces where varied species can bloom.

Dreams are the cutest! What's gone undreamed is even cuter.
In dreams I praise running rivulets, I praise the snowflake,
I praise the rainstorms which soak my clothes.
I praise those with less sorrow, praise them holding their bowls.
I praise those who tend to my security checks.
I praise the hard snowfall, the tender blossoms soon to come.
I praise my dinner, for the rib hidden beneath the braised wing.

Ezequiel Naya
de *Pueblos Para Escapar a la justicia*

translated from Spanish by Sam Simon
from *Villages to Escape from Justice*

A current of dread courses through the poems selected from Ezequiel Naya's *Villages to Escape from Justice*. Its characters resist relaxation, refusing to give themselves over to the notion of safety, connecting an unnamed past with an unknowable future, highlighting the uneasiness of those trading instability for unfamiliarity. What are these characters running from? Where are they going? While Naya makes a few references, the specifics aren't important. They could be about any one of Latin America's countries, cities, neighborhoods, homes, and families.

The collection explores the double-pronged mythology of nation-building and the desecration of those same countries, of the folklore and stories that both drive us towards war and help us survive it. They remind us of how those mythologies leave lasting impressions.

With the colloquial intimacy of a close friend and sharp disaffected humor, *Villages to Escape from Justice* examines the human cost of the decisions of those in power. That fallout ripples years or generations later during quotidian moments like drinking maté, lying in bed, or watering the plants, scrutinizing the fortitude it takes to live and love.

Guardan partes de su cuerpo
en casas de piedra.
No las venden ni las muestran.
Dos familias tienen sus ojos,
otros las piernas
unos pocos son felices
de tener un codo.
El amor, me dijo
cuando estaba entera,
es una planta que hay que regar

They keep parts of their body
in stone houses.
They neither sell nor display them.
Two families have their eyes,
others their legs
a few are happy
to have an elbow.
Love, she told me
when she was whole,
is a plant that must be watered

Pasábamos por la puerta sin decir nada. Baldosas rotas por hombres que nacieron en casas donde disparan. Algunos se animan a tomar la música del techo para después llevársela. La escuchan en los bosques, a orillas del río, y de a poco se sumergen hasta salir del otro lado. Se quedan perdidos y, por lo general, no vuelven. Aprenden un idioma nuevo, cambian de voz, de gestos, se cambian el color de ojos entre ellos. Regresan siempre y cuando haya sol. Sus padres los esperan con agua de lluvia entre las manos.

Al principio, se la pasan hablando del reflejo de la luz en las vías de alguna estación, y de cómo los trenes van y vienen sin gente. Después se ríen sin parar durante nueve horas porque quieren ser felices. Al final, se cansan y lloran. Cuando sienten que el mecanismo imperfecto de la máquina hará que todo empiece otra vez, toman las armas que guardan en la mesa de luz y disparan al techo para que la música suene.

We used to cross the threshold without saying anything. Tiles broken by men born in houses where they shoot. Some dare to take the music from the ceiling to carry away with them. They listen to it in the forests, on the banks of the river, and little by little they submerge themselves before reemerging on the other side. They get lost and, in general, don't return. They learn a new language, change their voice, their mannerisms, they swap the color of their eyes among themselves. They return always and as long as there's sun. Their parents await them with rainwater cupped between their hands.

At first, they spend their time talking about the reflection of the light on the tracks of some station, and how the trains come and go without people. Later, they laugh non-stop for nine hours because they want to be happy. In the end, they get tired and cry. When they feel that the imperfect mechanism of the machine makes it so that everything begins again, they grab the guns they keep in the nightstand and shoot at the ceiling to make the music play.

Fue cosa de irse a dormir sin viento. Tachado por lápices en documentos viejos que ya no se usan porque este país se hizo de nuevo y nadie quiere acordarse. Soñé que ya era abuelo y sacaba una silla a la vereda para sentarme junto a la puerta en una noche linda de primavera. Esas noches se van y así metemos las sillas adentro y nos refugiamos en ángulos de nuestras casas o departamentos. Vemos lentas las horas y el minuto de sol que se desmaya en el patio de atrás. Y el verano llega de nuevo. Los gordos muy gordos lo sufren pero en algún lugar del alma están contentos porque piensan que es mejor que esa gota en la cara sea sudor y no una lágrima por aquel país que deshicieron.

It was a matter of going to sleep without wind. Crossed out by pencils on old documents that they don't use anymore because this country was made anew and nobody wants to remember. I dreamed that I was already a grandfather and I took a chair out to the sidewalk to sit beside the door on a pleasant spring night. Those nights end so we put the chairs inside and take refuge in the corners of our houses or apartments. We slowly watch the hours and the minute the sun fades across the backyard. And summer comes once more. The very fat ones suffer but in some part of their soul they're happy because they think it's better that the droplet on their face is sweat and not a tear shed for that country that was dismantled.

POETRY FROM UKRAINE

Natalia Beltchenko

Kateryna Kalytko

POETRY FROM UKRAINE

There is a moment in *Chernobyl*, Craig Mazin's miniseries about the 1986 nuclear disaster, when the Soviet apparatchik in charge of the clean-up, Boris Shcherbina, orders the pilot of his helicopter to fly over the exploded reactor to survey the damage. "What we can't see we don't know," he growls. "Get us over that building, or I'll have you shot!" Seeing it is useless to point out the glow of radiation above the smoking rubble, Valery Legasov, the physicist appointed to assist Shcherbina, flings himself into the cockpit: "If you fly directly over that core, I promise you, by tomorrow morning you'll be begging for that bullet!" Not long after they watch from the ground as another helicopter, hovering to pour boron and sand over the core, silently disassembles and crumbles like dust in mid-air.

What we can't see we don't know. One would be hard-pressed to miss the resonance with the months leading up to the invasion of Ukraine in February 2022: resonance with Russia's absurdist denial of what has long been there for everyone to see (just last week Putin's foreign minister, Sergey Lavrov, was almost laughed off the stage at the G20, when he called the invasion a "war which we are trying to stop, which was launched against us") and with the appalling persistence of that denial in the face of its consequences, whose tragic scale we truly might never know. At the same time, Shcherbina's words also lift a hard mirror to years of minimizing and indifference on the part of Ukraine's allies, who looked on while fighting raged along its eastern border since the ousting of Viktor Yanukovitch in 2014. As though we really didn't know, until disaster finally forced us all to see.

In direct contrast with such wishful blindness, the contributions gathered in this section remind us that poetry subsists first and foremost on the resolve not only to see and to know, but to speak up in the face of violence and condescension. In a series of snapshots from her journey back to the Chernobyl Exclusion Zone thirty-three years after the explosion, Natalia Beltchenko balances an unflinching stare at the desolation of history ("Nothing is in the Zone") with all the lyrical energy necessary to see beyond it ("Exhaling the Chernobyl air— / A bird's song is heard"). Similarly, Katerina Kalytko pulls off the astonishing feat of pitching a loving, heartbreaking paean to the note of defiance that has become synonymous with the very name of her country around the world ("Good morning, greedy lord of carnage, / feeder of dogs, / piecemeal, I've approached you").

These are powerful words to fling into the cockpit, and I trust they will find readers ready and eager to listen to them. I am deeply grateful to Amelia Glaser and Yuliya Ilchuk, who worked with the poets to select these texts and translate them into English, for the opportunity to bring them to *Mantis*. I can hardly think of a better way to honor the journal's commitment to poetry as a voice for all the most difficult things—bravery, sanity, and therein truth and justice. Things we can't always see, and without which we'd all crumble like silent dust into the air.

Lorenzo Bartolucci
March 2023

Natalia Beltchenko
Ver Sacrum

Луб'янка — Іллінці

Сума смерті
в хатинці кожній згорьованій
в повітрі вдиху
Довге «у» як могильна яма
самум смерті пронісся
але самки в траві життя
народжують коників і коваликів
Довге «а» виструнчується
запліднює
Запилене
випиляне з ужитку

translated by Amelia Glaser and Yuliya Ilchuk
Ver Sacrum

Lubianka — Illintsi

The sum total of death
in every burnt hut
in the air a hooting howl
exhales a long "u" like the pit of a grave
the winds of death swept through
yet females in the grasses of life
give birth to beetles, grasshoppers
a drawn-out "aaa," tuning its strings,
fertilizes
pollinates
the dusty remains

Не відчіпляйте плуг
Ще не все поорано
Не лишайте.

Десь у Зоні відчуження
Долоня поля плине
В кишеню шукати лемеші —
І не знаходить

Don't unhitch the plow
There's still unturned soil
Don't just leave it.

Somewhere in the Exclusion Zone
The palm of the field reaches
Into its pocket in search of a plowshare —
And can't find it.

нонпарель
незрівнянні ліси луки річки
мохи птахи
два бики
в луб'янці
Полісся
по ліс я поліз
в зону
крізь моторошний шрифт
а там по-вітря колишнього
по вінця

nonpareil
incomparable woods meadows rivers
mosses birds
two bulls
in the village of Lubianka
the wooded Polesia
I scrambled through brambles
to the Zone
through that creepy typeface
and there was the before-wind
to the brim

річка Ілля
річка Бобер
річка Уж
Тепер
в зоні
Упричерть
з вужем і бобром
а Ілля не здичавів
тече тече тчк

in the Zone
the Ilya River
the Bober
the Uzh
now
fill and merge
with the eel and the beaver
and the Ilya didn't grow wild
it flows flows -(STOP)-

Село Бобер

тотемний звір бобер
то темний звір
Ніщо у Зоні
вилізло із нір
у Зоні — потяг попри
      страх
жене і обтинає зайве

Beaver Village

the beaver, totemic beast
is ever a bleak beast
Nothing is in the Zone
it's crawled out of holes
in the Zone desire in spite
of fear
pursues and removes the excess

Зона

Затягши, неначе у вирву,
Випліскує ззовні страхів.
Повітря чорнобильське видму —
Пташиний почується спів.

Усе, що здичавіти хоче
В мені — потонуло в луні.
Нізвідки повада уроча,
В нікуди виправи сумні.

Затерпнуть розвалені клуні,
Останні погаснуть вогні,
І простір на дівчину клюне,
Як єдиноріг у Клюні.

Є в Зоні щось від гобелена,
Доплетеного не завжди:
Весна в нього може священна
Землі поцілунок вплести.

The Zone

Having pulled me in, as if into a chasm,
It splashes me out of the terror.
Exhaling the Chernobyl air —
A bird's song is heard.

All that longs to run wild
in me has drowned in an echo
From nowhere — a magic charm,
To nowhere--sad missives.

Ruined barns will grow numb,
The last lamps will go out,
And this space will nuzzle the girl,
Like the unicorn at Musee de Cluny.

There's something of that tapestry
In the Zone, it's unwoven in places:
The rite of spring might still
weave in the Earth's kisses.

May 11-14, 2019

Kateryna Kalytko
Стояти до смерті

Отже, "стояти до смерті"
означає інколи саме це –
бути заживо порізаним на шматки.

Але як воно і чому, коли саме ти –
втілення лютої смерті
у світових новинах, клапоть шкіри
на канцелярському ножі,
між сторінками конвенцій,
конденсований біль, від якого
кишки чужі скручуються у вузол,
гарячі твіти, відео 18+,
розпластане, знерухомлене тіло,
чийого лиця не видно,
що від певної миті видає лише
тваринний хрип, розлюднюється;
нічне жахіття вцілілих, блювотні судоми,
дражливий контент.

Але також і ти –
різкий здивований крик народженого,
біг у високій прохолодній траві,
материн сміх,
ангіна, шкільні прогули,
жінка, з якою вперше кінчаєш,
жінка, яка від тебе вагітніє,
високе липневе небо,
гостра пам'ять про домашнє
ранкове світло,

translated by Amelia Glaser
Stand to Death

Well, "to stand to death"
sometimes means precisely this:
to be skinned alive.

But how can this be, when you yourself are
the furious death incarnate
in world news, a strip of skin
on a paperknife,
between pages of treaties,
condensed pain that
ties other people's intestines in knots,
trending tweets, age-restricted videos,
a prostrate, immobile body,
face blurred,
that emits only sporadic
animal gasps, dehumanizing;
a survivor's night terrors, convulsive vomiting,
sensitive content.

But you're also this:
a newborn's shrill, startled cy,
running through tall grass,
mother's laugh,
a sore throat, skipping school
the first woman you came with,
the woman you got pregnant,
a high July sky,
the sharp memory of home's
morning light,

прихована чоловіча беззахисність –
шкарубкі воєнні рукостискання,
жарти, вдалі та несмішні,
щось точне і невимовне
про любов,
алкоголь по вистудженому горлу,
спільна честь погибати.
Ім'я, обличчя.

Як воно – знати, що десь існують
вечори мерехтливого світла,
човни з нагрітими палубами,
сміх і цілунки,
діти хлюпочуться на мілководді,
десь наче зовсім поруч,
на іншому березі
калабані крові.

Затягніть міцніше на чорній плоті країни
турнікет кордону, крововтрата стає критичною.

Кожне скаже: він – це я.
І жодне не уявлятиме, як це насправді.
Як стиснуті зуби кришаться,
як згасає свідомість.
Ніхто не приходить сюди цілим,
аби бути розтятим.

Доброго ранку, зажерливий господи різанини,
годівниче песиголовців,
я шматками рушив до тебе.
Але ось ім'я. Розкажи тепер, спробуй,
у чому моя історія.

concealed masculine vulnerability
the calloused shell of a wartime handshake,
jokes that are funny and not
something precise and unspeakable
about love
alcohol on a congested throat,
the shared honor of dying.
A name, a face.

What's it like to know somewhere there are
evenings of twinkling light
boats with heated decks,
laughter and kisses,
kids splashing in shallow water,
somewhere as in really close,
on the other side
of the blood puddles.

Pull harder on the country's black flesh
border tourniquet, the hemorrhaging's becoming critical.

Everybody will say, "he's me."
And nobody will imagine what it's really like.
The way clenched teeth crumble,
the way consciousness fades.
Nobody comes here whole
just to be dismembered.

Good morning, greedy lord of carnage,
feeder of dogs,
piecemeal, I've approached you.
But here is my name. Now tell me, give it a try,
what's my story.

NEW POETRY

Janelle Cordero
Kyra Spence
Sarah Horner
Anon Baisch
Erika Kielsgard
M.P. Carver
Kenton K. Yee
Sarah Aziz
Ranjith Sivaraman
Emma Wells
Abigail Kirby Conklin
Corrie Thompson
Kevin Lemaster
Ariana Moulton
Tohm Bakelas
Emma Mooney
Enne Baker
Rajendra Persaud
Lily Kaylor Honoré
Niño Baena
Mehmet Kaan Eğretli
Aster Leonis
Pamela Wax
Selden Cummings
Alicia Shupe
Hrishikesh Srinivas
Jerrice J. Baptiste

Om Prakash Jha
Christine Neuman
Eileen Sepulveda
Heidi Seaborn
Kathryn Lauret
Hrishikesh Goswami
Lizzy Sparks
Sophie Hoss
Skylar Brown
Daisy Bassen
M. Cole
Peter Urkowitz
Tiara Dinevska-McGuire
Chandra Rice
Kevin Brennan
Serena Jacob
Anna Wright
Shane Ingan
Ruth Towne
James Kelly Quigley
Carolyn Kesterman
Christian Cacibauda
Robin Gow
Igor Kojadinović
Lawrence Bridges
Skylar Hendler
Aaron Nobes

Shanna Williams
Raymond Berthelot
Kyra Trumbull
Amanda Dettmann
Annie Cook
Cheyenne Hicks
Alex Stanley
Caroline Laganas
Nick Maurer
D. E. Kern
Felice Arenas
Thaddeus Rutkowski
Marcia Hurlow
Elizabeth Schmermund
Linds Sanders
Aritrika Chowdhury
Alejandra Hernández
Candice Phelan
Sheree La Puma

Janelle Cordero
Damn It All to Hell

Damn it all to hell, my dad says when something goes wrong, like the Toyota getting a flat or the dishwasher leaking or the drill running out of battery right before the screw is flush. He said it when I ran over a sprinkler head with the lawn mower as a kid and when I dropped a Lego castle from the balcony on the stairs and it shattered on the entryway tile into a million pieces, chipping the porcelain. He said it when I crashed the snowmobile into a pine tree and the dirt bike into a barbed wire fence. He said it when I backed my car into a post down at Ronnie D's Drive In just a week after getting my license. Damn it all to hell, he said when I didn't get the job I wanted, when someone stole my credit card, when my transmission failed on the highway. Damn it all to hell, he said when he tore the ligaments in his shoulder while rolling trusses for a spec house. Damn it all to hell, he said when his own father died, when he looked into the casket at the funeral and saw not the man he built homes with for sixty years but instead someone too small and sallow to be his dad, someone with blush on his cheeks and powder on his forehead and maybe even lipstick on his thin straight mouth. Damn it all to hell, I say now as my father's hair goes gray at the temples and we stand side-by-side staring at the mountain covered in cedar and golden larch, storm clouds building behind the peak, winter coming on.

Halloween, 1994

I was 4, my brother 6, and we wore Power Rangers costumes my mom
sewed herself from scraps of bright pink and red cotton. A few inches
of snow on the ground already, so my dad pulled us in a plastic toboggan
around the circle of our neighborhood. We wore boots and coats and
gloves that covered our costumes, but at least we still had our masks,
store-bought plastic molds with elastic strings that got caught in our
hair, holes for the eyes and mouth. At least our neighbors knew who
we were, or who we were trying to be: not the quiet kids at the top of
the hill who rode their bikes through the woods until dusk, but a pair
of superheroes saving the planet from space villains like Rita Repulsa
and Lord Zedd. We didn't complain about the cold even as we shivered,
even as nickel-sized snowflakes gathered on our shoulders and melted
on the crowns of our heads. We accepted handfuls of candy from each
grown-up with gracious bows and nods, knowing we were giving them
a gift, too. We were stoic when we got back home, eager only for sleep.
We hid our plastic pumpkins full of candy under our beds and dreamt
of galaxies far far away, of hand-fought battles under bright stars, of
victory.

Redneck Fountain

There's a boy of nine or ten lying face up and shirtless in the grass, skinny and white with a suntan, red basketball shorts down to his knees. Another kid of the same age stands a few feet from him with a green garden hose, and the water falls on the shirtless boy's chest and stomach. Both boys stay still and serene, like statues that make up a redneck fountain, a piece of art I understand without explanation because it's already familiar to me. I remember drinking from the hose on hot summer days as a child, the cold metallic water, dirt on the mouth. After, I'd always put my head under the stream until I got a brain freeze. Then I'd throw my long blonde hair over my shoulders and let the rivers of water trail down the back of my t-shirt as I rode my bike across the shimmering asphalt, sun on my arms and face but the inside of me still impossibly, magically cold.

Kyra Spence
Egrets on Route 41

When we get the news
we can do nothing about we are
standing on the side of the road
watching them.

Heat and heat. Black glass mud.
Burnt branches. A sensation
at the neck can reach everywhere.

Once hunted for their plumes,
wisped, glowing, white,
all the way to the brink. There
was one hunter who quit.

Over and over he saw the heads
the necks of them, naked,
hanging out of the trees by the

hundreds. Nest after nest,
featherless. I am done forever,
he said. He was not
the only one who saw it.

On this road before it was
a road. Six of them heave
up out of the watery prairie.

Wing flap, white broken
open in flight blur.

Hot, hot fields of water.
The rain holds.

I am listening so closely
to this scene
I am making up sounds.

Heat, wide open time.
One kind can reach
everywhere. It goes on.
It goes on. It does not go.

Sarah Horner
Cathedral, Crumbling

The God you forgot to pray to
is waiting at the end of the aisle,
disguised in emerald for ordinary time.
Your feet thump as you walk toward him,
a nerve-wracking echo reaching up at
the sky. Stained glass windows invite in
the light, creating a celestial mirage
that greets skeptical eyes.

Sweet-smelling incense tickles
the throat, stings the nose.
There is a strange sort of fog that
fills this cavernous space, this
place of relapsed time. It is
a gore and glory you cannot find
outside—a perpetual wanting
inside your half-changed mind.

When the angels sing their hymn,
you feel your body sinking through
dark wooden pews, returning to
the wormy earth beneath your calloused
feet. You wait for the seraphs to
reveal themselves—their white robes,
their gentle smiles. Behind the marble
alter they rise, wings battered but fine.

A stone-cold Jesus hangs below
the canopy, eyes shut and rolled up high.
Only half the candles flicker their light,

melting subtly on his either side.
It takes all your might to remain
upright—your knees and the floor
are like magnets; it's high time you
return to this nagging golden shrine.

Anon Baisch
my Mother died 29 days ago

Broken   the cellular the   definition
I   recognize   the   face   but

        Of   want   of   memory   of
                      But   I   need the   picture

Of   quickness   of erasure   Ashes
Of moment   of   seeing I

                              And the   could notting   we
                Of   invisible   touch   the   skin

Wait   wait   wait   wait   wait
Of   a moment   of   knowledge

                Do   we   know the   whenness
                    Of a   body   of   how

What is this   of ending
What is   this   finity   this

                          Stop stop   stop stop   stop
                          The   asymptote of body bag

The   asymptote of   and   the
Box   and   we must   carry

        And   we must   the lightness
                          What will   it feel   like

To   cradle   what   will feel
Cradle   cradle cradle   cradle   cradle

Erika Kielsgard
Orchis militaris

sì come schiera d'ape che s'infiora
una fïata e una si ritorna
là dove suo laboro s'insapora,

nel gran fior discendeva che s'addorna
di tante foglie, e quindi risaliva
là dove 'l süo amor sempre soggiorna.

—*Dante, Paradiso*

pottering in the chalk downs
captured my imagination

tree-muffled evening
inverted wishful thinking

village hills today a garden suburb
tang of seaweed romantically remote

I lived in hopes, another insect
haunting thyme-scented silence

half-believed in holidays
hung over me, withered in the bud

flowers were my first love
and seem likely to be my last afternoon

the scattered stars of pink anemone
mere memories of memories

*

not always there, flower names
are oddly interchangeable

archetypal pictures of a bee
in blue Bengal light

belonging partly to the vegetable
I joined as a private

abstracting faculty absent
one miracle repeated

a sense of reality
the Head already preparing

for the sacrifice
appearing sporadically

comet by accident
yet to come

*

anyone can write nonsense
about flowers

artificial paradises
prick with tears

resounding names
typical of a poet's botany

a vague reference to violet
omissions in jam pots

upholstered imagery
of long purples

vascula crammed
historical parentheses

curiously heart-shaped
holes still unfound

*

fading flowers unrequited love
the discovery made me

sunlit for weeks
transfigured, fringed

fabulous lineaments
unmitigated relief

cylindrical spike, broader
divisions of the lip

annihilating consciousness
of future fallen plums

barriers burnt golden
a new wallpaper

where orchids lurked
he took my hand

*

damp expanse of skin
flowering in the waste patches

the wine bottle gleamed darkly
never-to-be-repeated lyric

unseasonable architecture
springing nakedly

taken for some ruined temple
few windows left intact

sky-blue irises conceal nothing
grave behind his spectacles

sudden leaf overnight
I looked again

dried skeletons of windless morning
stealing up like tiny birds

M.P. Carver
You Have Secrets but They're Nothing Special

Radio signals float over the bay,
whisper to the swelling waves.
The chimney bricks quake slow,
wiggling free from their mortar.
Under the leaves, those oaks
splay themselves against the sky.
When she can no longer sleep,
the cat spends her days twisting
around her own spine—
in her mind she strategizes
a reprieve from birdsong.
She lays love down the first chance
she gets, turns off the lights,
and heads for war.

Quiescent

It's Sunday and the rain passes through me on its way into the ground.
These tiny dogs I'm watching are alien creatures full of needs
I can't speak to. Day by day they walk the same streets,
sleep in the same spots, seem to suffer the same appetites.
My life grows small like theirs, scrambles up the back porch
with its angular mountain of steps. Beyond my peripheral
some world is turning, I could see its shadow if only I switched on
the radio or the tv or my phone or my laptop or Alexa—even the
    thermostat
sees more of this world than I do, yearns to feed me little pieces of it.
The dogs sleep while I start dinner, the smart fridge screen dark
but humming, aching to join the cat's cradle of connected things.
If I woke everything up could I say the house was breathing?
Wanting? Same as the little dogs? Same as me? For now,
we are closed off and quiet—a chamber for this smothered day.

Your Hat

For the lady at the grocery store

Your Hat casts a
shadow on the whole world,
it's an upside-down kingdom peopled
by the red spaghetti of your hair which floats
around the town on top of your cloud-high noggin.
Your Hat is woven from discount sun-bleached dreams,
the well-worn ones you've been repeating for years. Here
in the Trader Joe's, Your Hat goes to battle with the cantaloupe

and a calvary of lilies, and by God I think Your Hat might just win. Your Hat is
a conundrum of incompatible coupons and unamused store clerks working their last
week on the job. Your Hat leads you out the door, and I'm on the stage of a Greek
tragedy, alone among the wine-dark cheeses—in an aisle starved for shade

Kenton K. Yee
It's Accrual World

If you work 7, commute 2, sleep 7, and waste 7 hours
today, how much time is left to pursue what you like?
To change your life, sometimes a little math is all you need.
I know, you're a humanist / artist / leader,
above bothering with math or manual labor.
Me too.
A dose of fuzziness every day keeps the actuary away.
Even mathematicians have flirted with fuzzy numbers,
i.e., 'garbage' in lay terms / 'nonsense' in literary terms.
Painters / poets / presidents / marketeers have popularized
nonsense with success. The trick is to ground
88% nonsense in 2% truth and 7% beauty.
A little makeup goes a long way.
As every brown bear knows, garbage is 63% refuse,
12% compost, 25% recyclables, and 69% delicious.
The squirrel refuses a dandelion head
but gobbles up your apple core. Hello, goodbye.
Pi never stops while 3.1415926 times zero is zero.
This is the difference between truth and beauty
if you want to know the truth / beauty of it.

Sarah Aziz
father tongue

The Bengali Language Movement was a political movement that began in what is today known as Bangladesh, in an effort to recognise the use of their mother tongue as an official language after India's partition in 1947 and to retain its writing in the Bengali script.

On 21 February, 1952, the police killed seven students from the University of Dhaka demonstrating for the movement.

the moon spills seven white
-hot tears over the shore of this sea
-facing city with no beach and
you say your forgiveness is
insurmountable as you make me
stumble over my own mother's
knees. i paint my tongue with
mustard oil hoping to cough
out her name as you
sneer sympathetically. i am
worth half your soil, my hair
coiling at the edges like all your
goddesses as i watch an old
man painting their scarlet-rimmed
eyes glassy like my plea, his spotted
forehead a reminder of
what could have been
in the arms of my grandfather, for
the weight of an unrecorded riot is not
half as heavy as a ten-year-old big brother's

broken vow and the God i kneel
before still hasn't shown me how
to look less like the father you say
has never been mine.

Ranjith Sivaraman
Moments without You

Moments without you
Have cute little teeth,
And my heart still tender
My soul still wonders.
For every bite
A flower blooms,
A tear weeps
and rolls down fragrant,
I taste and my sigh
Flies into an afar sky.

Emma Wells
Countess

I made the headlines,
spotted, caught on camera;
modern day smartphones
are my nemesis,
stalking me with flashy filters,
showcasing Tudor dresses
disharmoniously in 2022 images;
the press rumble,
print a half-name,
clutching at straws,
tendrils of identity,
slinking as pondweed
through curious fingers.

Previous centuries were easier:
I'd hover in moonlight,
glide staircases leisurely,
portrait myself in framed windows,
run ghostly hands over bridges
to no recognition, no clicks,
but now technology cloisters me
sinking me to darkened depths,
where I wallow in the moat
like a rusted penny
dropped into a wishing well
curling with enraged roots.

My figure tells my shame,
a rounded eight-month belly
protrudes from swelling tides

with the ghoul of a newborn
perpetually encircling my womb
as a ghostly coiled snake;
its skin has shedded many times
always growing back
as blooms of a first kiss
in my shrouded memory.

The unborn hates me…

I sense her distaste
spinning in a circuitous jail
bruised by watery shackles
bored beyond belief:
restless as a flightless heron,
talons mud-slick thick,
frowning in dismay.

The night I flung myself
blinded by infatuation
from the twisted tower,
jilted, loved no longer
while he writhed with a new lover
amidst hot-sweat sheets;
no longer holding his gaze -
love splintered, fractured to shards
like my handheld mirror
dissipating to glassy echoes.

I couldn't swim,
I planned it all.

In the afterlife,
I course the moat
like a hellfire nymph

dispatching flecks of flames
in my watery wake;
I float, waterborne
as a damnable fairy,
weightless, supernatural.
as the stirrings in the west-wing…

Media interest piques
brewed by my frenzy,
so sightings multiply.

I turn over new leaves…

Prolonged despondency mutes
no longer festering
in darkened depths
wallowing and water-weary;
I now smile at the camera
cherishing attention
growing boldly boisterous,
relishing the limelight
(pretending to be coy)
as I twirl golden Tudor threads
between reawakened fingers.

Abigail Kirby Conklin
La Nouvelle Cuisine

It is a relief to know
of the marrow
in the bones
in the legs
of a cow
long left
in a field.

That I could crack
in, knife in
hand, hard;
unearth
some
thing
alive.

That a year could turn
overhead, sky
tumbling
black
to blue
to midnight
mouth open
to a sun, and again

and
I could
still be here;

guilty-breathless,
steaming with blood
satiated and grinning.

Seasonal Kool-Aid

It is fall
and my teeth are limned
with the grit
of the sugar
of the trees
committing suicide
during the annual Jonestown
massacre of deciduous
lawn-ornaments
that is the season.
If I lie down
beneath the one guy's
maple on Shaw
will he construct
a little gravestone
for the tree and I?

Here lies some woman
I found rolling
around on my lawn
as the season forced
my tree to sleep.

Rest in Peace
this white girl
and the dropped dress
of my sugar maple
fallen about her.

In Memoriam
of the neighbor

who stopped here
and said "enough"
and the sun-bellied
red shroud
of the maple
cupped her
in its palm,
sang her to sleep.

Corrie Thompson
Relentless

The waves keep coming
Like love they knock me
      Into their same,

And I skin my knees
Sun's fire dripping
Salt screaming
      Over my voice
Yanked to and fro
In the undertow
Which baby turtles throw
Themselves into

Moon's gravity rows
Over shore
An offering of shells
Plump gulls and plovers
Fight over

I extract myself,
Labored breath mentioning
Death like a homecoming

Not today, I say
Forcing myself upright
In the sand

Ghost crabs rambling
Across dry shadows

Small, excavated piles
Flung from their residence

My stringy hair *thwacks* my back
My teeth crunch on the grit
        Of eaten words

Foam roams up to my ankles
Soothing my fatigue
The heat returns in shame
        To my cheeks

My weaknesses tested and bested
By repetition—which some
Claim as insane, but I see
As the only way to hope,

To swim out far enough
To the sand bar,
To see reefs of polyps
        And starfish,
To glimpse beneath
The surface of a dream,
To star on the stage
        Of delirium,
To wage war against yourself
        For love

The relentless waves
Will not cave into our needs,
But shape up,
Shape Earth,
Revealing secrets
        Shell by shell
And swell in pride
When we endure

Kevin LeMaster
10,000 Hours (or the time it takes)

Someone once said that's how long
It takes to   be good at

     Anything   like poetry
I started late   destined in my forties

to be still trying at seventy   experienced already
in dying   life   and children

I have the art of walking   down   with a precision of
Steps   and movement that mimic

A waltz without music   and talking
Was a birth of love

like a train pulled from
a tunnel   all that sound

pulsing with life

a unique practice   of love
    unrequited   stings like

Ripping flies   from their wings
making me an artist   of sorts

Now   being great at poetry
    Will have to wait till I almost
forget   what it is like

To be so clever   forget alliteration
Or rhyme   or song

10,000 hours   27 years   maybe ill be
as great   as a flower in   an empty field

Or a proof set   of 1965 quarters
Giving you   one   more   day

glistening   when the light hits me
just right

Ariana Moulton
Out of Office

You can't hear it
when the moon's
limb passes through
the Earth's shadow.
It doesn't tell you
what it's going to do.
It doesn't warn you
that your eyes will
seem to play tricks,
and this lunar eclipse,
this blood moon
is a paper collage.
Nighttime scissors
snip a sliver of
wax paper,
big enough to
cover one eye,
big enough to
reveal change
you didn't know
was folded into a leaf
or a ballot, ink stained
with tomorrow's bodily
laws writing themselves
across the sky.
It's as if God himself
held the moon in his mouth,
tricking you into believing
you could repair all of this.

One piece of scotch tape at a time.
Reaching through the open window,
telling the stars to hide,
for they could be next in
line to vote the moon
out of office.

Tohm Bakelas
tohm bakelas plays poetry

I'd rather be Richard Speck
than Gary Snyder - David Lerner

i want to be a poet but
i don't want to be a poet,
do you understand?

i want my name written
in smoke across blue skies
and carved upon the backs
of immortal sparrows and
seared into the fractured minds
of the living and the dead

i want my words chiseled
into the sides of empty buildings
that serve no purpose but
to take up space so that
people passing by can
have a reason to complain

i want my words planted
in the screaming mouths
of drought-stricken flowers
that beg for rain beneath
the merciless burning
august sun

i want to be a poet but

i don't want to be a poet,
do you understand?

i once believed that to be a great poet
you had to publish every damn poem
you wrote and that anything less
was considered failure

i once filled my nights with writing
as many poems as possible
and not giving a shit if any
of it was good or decent

now i write my poems by rewriting
the same fucking lines
i wrote years ago,
just somewhat
slightly different

now i take my poems,
and beat them like a dirty rug,
drag them through streets
like a disobedient dog,
let them incubate while
i catch my breath and
sleep off the hell

there is no right way to do it,
everyone does it differently,
do you understand?

every poet i read is dead,
they all sought something greater
that ended in suicide

i have a masters degree in social work

and the highest clinical license
in the state of new jersey,
but it's not literature
it's not poetry

i barely follow rules and fight with
clenched teeth against bureaucracy
that sticks hot knives into my hands
and bandages up the damages with
the promise of a pension at 63 years old,
but it's not literature
it's not poetry

new jersey has not elected me
the poet laureate of the state,

new jersey has not given me
grants to be a poet

new jersey doesn't give a fuck
about me or my poetry

and why should they, do you?

Emma Mooney
Wild Swimming

Lipstick left at home,
no vanity here.
These wild wimmin smash
the looking glass.

Lady Hall

She sits by the fire, stitching the last pocket
onto her white nightdress. It's a new moon
tonight.

On the beach, blonde curls rush towards her,
bouncing. Small fingers clutch brightly
coloured pebbles.

She must hurry, the stone steps leading
into the sea will soon disappear. The tidal pool
was cut out of the rocks by her husband's men
as a wedding gift.

She slips a perfectly round, white pebble
into her pocket. The children never arrived.
None of her babies made it to full term.
This is where she came to bathe. After.

Pockets full, she walks, barefoot, into the cold
salt water. The waves tug at the hem of her
nightdress, calling her to join them. A gull
cries in the sky above.

Enne Baker
Star Scars

You drew stars around my scars,
And now I'm bleeding, and the blood exiting
My galactic wound is eating itself into a
Blackhole by leaving.

I can count my lucky stars,
That I have you giving me your
Weekends to do this for me.
Spring breaks loose;

It's nightfall; the stars are evident
In this kind of hour.
I live and die for moments that we stole,
As we grew grey and old,

Sleeping in for half a day,
Gay and sad,
We can call it even.
I was read by you many times,

To the point, you became dead,
Like a shooting star,
You couldn't interpret my wishes anymore.
So you decide to place yours onto mine,

As I grant them, and you take them for granted,
So I grant the wishes of the old scars you drew on
Me, connected with a marker to its
Healed parts and filled its space to transcend.

Rajendra Persaud

Pink Sherbet Meridian, or the Evening Razzmatazz in the West

she scalps native bubbles,
soapy water splatters
like forbidden glitter on the brow
of a hardened man
renamed "Pop-Pop"
without consent.
you dare touch the gold tooth,
the one we never would.
giggles, clears his raspy throat.
"Enough"!
he rises,
running back
at first whimper.

napkin love note

The key to a good love letter
is timing

oh, and also
the right audience.

The key to a good love letter
is your confidence
in affection's return.
Unrequited love is ambition's death.

oh, and also
your words.

A good love letter
isn't a text message,
it's flowy cursive
exasperated scribblings
signed with x's and o's
and hearts
the author filled in
[him]/[her]self
with perspiration from trepidation.

oh, and also
maybe a theme?

A love letter can be
as simple as
macaroni and glue
if it's from you.

oh, and also
a powerful motif or a memory.

A love letter is
a piece of your soul
manifest on paper.
Soul left behind?

oh, and also
a plot?

Actually, it shouldn't be *that* long.
The plot is your story
yet untold.

A love letter is the
saddest truth
you muster.
I'm sorry you had to write it,
that you thought the recipient
didn't already know.

oh, and also
glitter

A love letter unopened is
a suicide note.

Lily Kaylor Honoré
Mathematics of Grief

Karolyn buys three jumping spiders
from a masked woman in a parking lot
so that she is not the only living being
in her mother's house.

When she comes back home next month
San Francisco will be the only place named *home*.
Pledge spiritual fealty to SF drag queens, yes,
swim far to the far coast,
but Louisville, Kentucky was the undertow.
Back there, there was always
a place to sleep, a car to drive, food in the fridge.
Her mother. There was always her mother.

Karolyn says, anything she does not take now
from her mother's house
will not exist.

When your mom goes. Passes. Passes away.
(No one says dies.)
Dorothy plots quitting her job again:
>   *I thought I was fine*
>   *but I'm really not.*
I tell her, it won't be linear.
Do I mean geometric, algebraic?
It'll be a bumpy line of 1970s rickrack
ridges and troughs.

Sound Translation

In my sister Isolde's car crossing the Bay Bridge,
we are two adults and two children, masked.
Driving to our mom's driveway,
Thanksgiving 2020, we will outdoor-gather,
we will household-mingle, for the first time.

In the passenger seat I've got my camera out,
photographing her, the sky, 360-degree stimuli:
Isolde, two feet away, not through a computer screen!
Velocity of billboards and blue sky and needlenosed buildings
coming at me through the windshield,
so much bigger than laptop Netflix!
I'm taking pictures of the steel beams overhead
and banditface selfies in the side mirror as we rush eastward;
windows rolled down whip my words away as I say

    I haven't seen water in a while.

This whole year I'd only walked, no trains cars or buses.
Landlocked in a coastal city. Neighboring cities
turned stagecoach distant, turned future tense.
After a pause   (she always pauses before she speaks,
        like our father, how this tic of an inheritance
        when he never lived with us?)   she says

    Yes, you haven't seen her since March.

I say *water*, she hears *mother*.
Our mother, the water,
universal,
larger than the bay, the sea, the tide.

our mother the water   the water the mother
watermother   motherwater   la mère la mer
themotherthesea   the mother sees
mother   mother

Mother?

Thanksgiving. Lap dinner on the steps
at the top of the steep driveway
three small sororal households
stationed ten feet apart.
We wave and Andy makes a joke and
the kids fall off plastic chairs and
I spritz rubbing alcohol on my mother's hands
and she pours us champagne.
I'm so happy I'm crying.

Thanksgiving. A few weeks back
Karolyn's mom told the nurse
she wouldn't be here for Thanksgiving
and she wasn't.
She passed the night before.

Thanksgiving.
Karolyn's first day
motherless.

Dorothy's first holiday
        alone here.

Alyx's first holiday
        not anywhere.

Towards the end, once,
Karolyn's mom didn't recognize her.
Hearing that, I feel crumpled.
Please forget this last bit, lethe waters rising.
You don't want to know
that your mother does not know you.
Remove. Roll back.
Only a dream,
not the true true.

Niño Baena
Black and White Reels (II)

In the moonlight
I followed the white dog

as I emptied myself
of pubs, I visited

the graves of my ancestors:
Baudelaire Vallejo Cioran

at dawn
with the shadow

behind me
the church bell bellowed

like a cow
being slaughtered

the fluffy white mutt peed
on the dark side

of the wall
and these staggering ruins

of Europe
I moved into

avoiding any messiah

Mehmet Kaan Eğretli
When a Soldier Sighs

The turning of almighty earth,
The flirting of stars above us,
The hell cannon that thunders
And turns separate flesh into clusters
Of meat and bloody dirt,
It all stops,
When a soldier sighs.

Dull heads decorated,
Stories of lands pissed and marked,
And those ununique voices begged
By the beggars buckled in trenches
Being boiled in a pot of perfect plans,
When a soldier sighs,
Turn insignificant.

The voice of other's tongues
Stabbing into the breast, while laughs
Besiege the painfully bold brain,
When compared to the sigh of a soldier
As the bayonet rips through the sinews of his hearth,
Sounds quiet.

Storms that took the mighty ship
And flung it to the sides of mountains
Flooded by His will, nor cries countless
Barked by rotting war-makers as they drowned,
Could neither startle an infant's hip,
When compared
To a soldier's sigh.

Lashing brother unto brothers,
Sons unto fathers,
Heavens cruded by disasters
Tempest-stricken will lie,
He who cast the shadows
Of war in men
Pharaohs ordering slaught as pharaohs were to die
When the faint firing squads
Whereby they achieved reign
Turn against them,
When their no-good tongues
Simmer in blood and phlegm,
When sighs rock the cradle of Bethlehem,
Will see, when the bullets ground their fattened thighs,
If men are gaps to fill, what makes a soldier sigh.

Aster Leonis

Respite

The cold beam of the February sun
Shining on my face
The birds are singing around me
I feel my lungs expand as I reach
For the first breath in days
I can even discern my thoughts
And suddenly it seems like there is no war
Like everything was a nightmare
But soon the blasts will start again
The news will pour again
And this fake stillness
Will evaporate into thin air
Like did our lives from before
From which only remains a distant taste
It was only a couple of days ago
But I feel so old already
Time is relative to the will of the tyrants
And maybe tomorrow time will stop
Completely
It already has for so many
And so, I listen to the birds
I hope I will be here again tomorrow
I hope
They will be too

Pamela Wax
If You're Lucky

You love that Jane Goodall
writes about hope, despite
all the bad news on your doorstep
like a million species as sitting
ducks on their way to extinction.
You get nature's lust to re-create
itself—how the peregrine falcons
re-nested after the black
air in Sudbury, how the nuked
oleanders in Hiroshima revived,
how the octopus grows
a new arm, the skink a new tail.
But your mind does loop de loops
around Jane's faith in the human
will to resurrect ourselves.

If you're lucky, most of life
is boring. You get
up every morning to pee,
turn on the tea kettle,
Zoom through your day.
Sometimes that humdrum
is punctured by breaking news:
an unprecedented storm
bolting up the coast, another
insult from clogged chambers
of Congress, a novel variant
of despotism, or a text
from a friend about her diagnosis.

You recount these aberrations
on your weekly phone calls
with distant relatives, rehash
false memories of good ol' days
on the levee, where Archie
was just some fiction in Queens,
not the guy behind the deli
counter at Safeway who gives
your BLM t-shirt stink eye.

You'd rather shine light—
like Jane—in the nooks
of possibility, slow
dance with faith
in the One above,
face down fear that this
will be the day the music
dies, confident
in the radiating powers
of your friend's treatment—
happy for a while, joking
full throttle with the guy
behind the deli counter.

Selden Cummings
Hyssop

You say you found me in the river.
Did my silence call you?
Infants have such a way with women.
I recall gray shadows resting on gray water,
  bulrushes flanking the riverbanks, cicadas
  speaking unseen, rubbing jagged legs between
  jagged blades of grass.

I recall more than you.
Not more than you recall but more than you,
  yourself.
I can taste the clover when I close my eyes.
The way the man's flesh finally split, like an overripe
  fruit, how oil on leather shines differently than oil
  on my sister's hair.

Once I coaxed a cat onto a flat raft and
  pushed it down the river.
I watched until I couldn't hear it any longer.
Your father has told me that love is a bureaucracy.
I don't believe him
  but he is a beautiful man.

You cared for me when I hit my head on the stone buried
  in the mud alongside the game trail, and the rain
  made us all sick.
You said pneumonia or tuberculosis took the servants. I asked
  which, and you said that it did not matter.
I slept for two weeks and had visions of a vast desert, a red

wasteland cracked by ancient upwellings, water's footprints
fossilized to taunt the dying wanderer.

That I might walk across this river
    I pray, that I might pull the waters back
    like muddy curtains, or even walk upon
    its surface, I pray.
I know you won't understand these things. The shadows. The cat.
The distant mewling. I know that I should thank you, but I'm not sure
how.
Royalty is a trick of the light. The people fear me, though
    even after all these years
    I am terrified to look upstream.

Alicia Shupe
Part of Me

Wishes
that it were only May
twenty-five,
and we had another month
of life,
in this city.
Another month to walk
in the dark
'round the city seat
at night.
To play full-moon
Peter Rollins
bingo,
and drink, wonder
whiskey or stout.
To laugh and think,
"Wasn't it only yesterday
you didn't know my name?"

Part of me wishes
we'd lived beyond July
five,
unknown days
lived in
unknown spaces.
Soundless,
empty nights
stretched
            endlessly
across grassy skies,

against too far stars
                  and
silent
highways, east
to hometown,
  goodbye
love.

Hrishikesh Srinivas
Swallowed

When my font is bold and full I feel on-edge worse than
artless as though it were out of my hands
although it is I who write. In expressions of others
re-writ, in sound that has been well-produced
I sing along to in the vague hope of finding a tone – mine.
But really I give up swimming days on-end barely float
to await the uncertain swelling current I cannot want
but I surround myself I am me I am the sea
so who determines to carry myself to safety?
Even as legs stiffen to lead and the neck twists
to suck an ever chopped-up air whose unwanted
isolates mirroring dig into their side? Yet no glance
over one shoulder reviewing diluted appearances.
At some point it will seem very different to how
it seems now – that is the way of a point, *it seems*
twists things, and yet how many words unwind the spirit
that knows to express itself even in checks and balances
even if in doing so it may drown. There its truth
in moments meant for stealing, exposed, pain off the back
meant to be lost "with pleasure", like tossing sheaves sun-glinted
from balconies up to hear the sound of something carried
like the body's carried by limbs, like bones feathers air pockets,
so on pages that admit their dissolute expression
another denuding of selves; there its worth, it to fall
to be swallowed, to let cave in what would seem only light…
If I have thought about those words that pour
and the words that mock that they cannot,
about seekers' and sought-afters' and value-mongers',
of all I read or heard my spirit kept a few alone, seeming

always from long ago to call dear whether they pour now or not
and running back, cloth at half-mast, stringers into water, water
into ocean, ocean to which I can only guess these rivers
run: this metaphor, this like, excuses what it cannot witness
would lock itself in with the sea itself and switch it on...
In all the blazing flood that engulfs my spirit, my word,
how could my word end in such comfort derelict?

Jerrice J. Baptiste
November Light

Late November morning light pierces
through tumultuous clouds.

A dusting of snow hugs green grass.
Seasons transitioned effortlessly before

cruelty from human hands and mind.
May the earth forgive us. We can only ask.

We're still mourning plastic bags.
We do know this earth is a tapestry. Home

to icebergs reflecting on periwinkle seas.
Home to hummingbirds, elephants, fields of lemongrass.

Many species of animals & plants divorced this earth.
Only grace can wed us to new growth. Have mercy

When your fingers touch lilies in soil. Dream a dream
of delicate ecosystems because we care.

Om Prakash Jha
Old-broken-drums

Hanging from my neck
an old-broken-drum is being beaten
sometimes by known hands
sometimes by unknowns hands,
I try to beat a new drum
in my own rhythm that springs
from heart-beats
my rhythm is the splash of my blood
        it's the sound of my breaths
        it's the echo of my soul
        my rhythm is me,
Alas! Each time others appear
and beat my drum ruthlessly.

My neck refuses to carry it
but some men come
and try to convince my neck
to bend down,
they forget that for a genuine rhythm
neck must be straight
eyes must be clear
and hands mustn't be fake.

Treading through bent necks
dusty eyes
and fake hands,
makes my walk difficult.

After a great effort

I erase and wipe out the mosses
that had made the pavement slippery,
in the meantime
a warbler from New York Forest
crossing the sky over 'The Statue of Liberty'
and putting its beak near my ears
whispers a note of love,
and I, as an eagle, flutter my wings,
then fly high in the sky
the old drum falls down
in a war field
and breaks into pieces,
the fights and skirmishes stop.
now they know
they are fighting for the redundant
for yesterday,
not for the new
not for tomorrow.

A flamingo in Europe dances,
I see an old petal, in its beak,
collected from Kiev just before the war.

Thank you warbler!
I'll continue to erase and wipe out
mosses seen on dilapidated embankments
I'll continue to throw out
old-broken-drums
hanging from bent necks.
Good bye! Old-broken-drums!

Christine Neuman
Decomposable

I went to my best friend's mother's funeral.
I guess *I've reached that age.*

DJ threw his cash app card on top
of the coffin as it descended
into the ground.

I hate desk jobs.
I hate customer service jobs.
I love jobs that don't pay well.

Peach fuzz, frontal sex.
I thank God for them both.

I've been sitting on the left side of my bed
for so long that I decided to move
to the far right corner today,

the song of my childhood.

I don't know the language they speak there,
but I'm going to the Comedy Club
in East Sacramento anyway.

I cleaned my car. I cleaned my room.
I can still smell remnants of you
masking the bleach and dust.

I am drinking tea
and my skin is burning

with the sensation that I might not
leave this place forever.

Eileen Sepulveda
New York City Windows

Damp windowsills
Icicles melting
Raindrops
It's the blizzard from New Year's Eve
Snow mountains are ashtrays and
Next door neighbors
Are lovers quarreling and
Mothers screaming and
Children crying
Cars parked
No one is moving
No Sunday church processions
Get the warm gloves out
The hooded sweaters
"There's gonna be mo' money, next year" Daddy always says
Like leaves falling
By the wooden bedpost
Eggs splattered on New York City Windows
Halley's comet never made it to the South Bronx
Aurora skies as my eyes start to close
Dreams of
Solar systems colliding
Like fireflies in the summertime
The thick linen curtains are still up
And the smell of wet paint lingers
"Say goodnight, you must go to bed now," Mommy says
Daddy's coming home soon
His wet sneakers will be
Drying on the sill

Heidi Seaborn

Hear Hear the Devil is Near

~with a line from Lawrence Ferlinghetti

We were putting up a statue. Stone-
faced like winter, I watched, arms
crossed, listening in my tone-
deaf way. We were pulling on the rope—
the heft of church bells. Everything
ringing, I uncrossed my heart,
walked back. You can't unsee.
There was a fellow who asked
what we were up to?
What were we up to—a genuflective
reflex? A board game of God &
Monuments? When the pastor came
round for tea, I knew I'd been made.
Naturally, there's always a bit of theatre.
Consider the way hands become
shadow birds in the bright afternoon sun,
the power of shining a torch
into the dark corners. Blink blink.
Let's give it a think my mother
said when I bolted like a horse
or wore the short skirt of sacrilege.
But now we're getting somewhere—
maybe it's a church square
or the cemetery out back, a stone's
throw from City Hall. Turn right
at the statue. Or kiss the cloak—
lips slipping words into the hem—
like my fellow patriots who've all gone
mad. That's what taking down

a statue can do. Even the church
goers in their Sunday best, blessed
by God & Monuments are damned.
I often think of what to ink
on my body. But I can't undo.
So why not stay plain Jane, skin
like a white altar cloth? And then
the Holy Trinity comes to me—
sweet Jesus—like a spirit really.
What could I do but tramp stamp
the Holy trifecta? Carry
the burden of being baptized
into the communion on conspiracies.
We were raising the flag like an Olympic torch—
wearing white togas & Nikes. Everything
moving so fast, swept up. But I slept in,
alarms ringing. You can't unknow. Again,
we were pulling on a rope—
the heft of church bells. Everything
ringing. You can't unhear
the church bells? Hear
them ringing?

Kathryn Lauret
Home

I was raised by a therapist and a hospital chaplin
So I know there are no bad people just hurt people
My mom told me about a client of hers who broke his own cheekbone with a
hammer because he thought his face would scare his family
I was twelve but I too was beginning to find monsters in the mirror
My dad told me about a boy who broke his brain in a skateboarding accident.
He lost the ability to lie and told my dad about a shadow that gave him
the option to stay or go
I don't know if my dad believes in God, I think he believes in the same things I do.
My little brother is a Gemini, an understanding devil's advocate. Sometimes his
patient logic can calm me down just enough.
I make homes out of the people I fall in love with
Right now my home has many doors
I try to take my time in the halls
Unwilling as I am for my own hinges to creak
It's been a year and he says
There's more of us to discover
But how do I articulate all this truth in my eyes?
Loving each other was only the first chapter
Now we will uncover all the reasons why this connection holds us together like
rain rushing to the earth
My life will be built out of these trials and treasures
So many years left to create myself
While sharing it all with the roof over my head
In the elementary school where I am paid to spend my days
Children are scared because they think life will always be like this
My job is to help them through and try not spoil the surprise

Pink Clouds

Love bled out of him
Like blood from a bullet wound
I knew before he said it
Thursday night in the empty bar
Drunk like I told him not to be.
I remember how it hurt all summer
To walk away from him
Before the prophecy in his eyes came true
Didn't know I was right
About everything I knew.
Love is paid in attention, I believe
And the first night in my bed
He noticed every one of my 16 tattoos.
Such a sweetheart when he's sober
Devil's downfall as a drunk
Face so serious as I talk slow
Listening because it's all he can do
Doesn't waste our time with promises
We both know he'll do it again
We both know he'll fix it again
Actions speak louder than words
So I've heard.
They should see the way he watches me
As I drive us through the night
Faces glowing in the street light
His hand warm in mine
They should see the way he runs to me
All through his days
Like there's no option to stay away.
He says he thinks of me
When the sky turns pink

Winter skies with cotton candy clouds
Every night this week.
I wouldn't want him to hide
The blue in his green
If anything it makes him
All the more human
Can't count it as a crime to be alive
I am witnessing a forest fire
Destruction is a natural cycle
But he thinks he can stop
I stand in the way
Catching him on a heavy gaze
Beautiful with strength
Reflecting red in my eyes
I've been searching for years
For this kind of light.

Hrishikesh Goswami
The White Crease

A keen white line
Ran confidently
Across the dark blue firmament

Quite clear
Quite sharp
Too smart to catch
To uninviting to explain
Too tough to apprehend

Is the meaning of this very crease

Lizzy Sparks
decompose with me

love, let us lay together here in this wet earth.
let it consume us. let it sink its teeth into our soft flesh.
let the earth swallow us whole, eat us raw.
let us return from that which we came:
for we are not ashes to ashes, dust to dust.
we are earth to earth, we are earth from earth.

i do not know of eternal life but i know of
your hand in mine. so let us lay here.
the seasons will change. soon it will be spring and
moss will grow
where your spine once was
flowers will bloom
in the decay of my ribcage

let us create an eternity for ourselves
here among the bogs here laying
among the peat and moss and sundews
let it blanket us. let us become one with the dirt.
here we will welcome death. i am no longer afraid
for they will find us hand-in-hand

i speak of decay, but decay is not a guarantee.
this is an act of
preservation:
the acid of the peat
will melt our bones
but not the flesh.
not the organs.
they will find my heart
one day and know it beat with yours.

Sophie Hoss
View from the Bridge After Snow

Ice pins the ocean
and the water writhes,

splintering frost the way
a bite ruptures the gloss of sugar

on candied apples.
I've sometimes wondered

if it would feel good to
smash a glass snow-
globe on the floor.

Skylar Brown
Venice Beaches

I went to Venice and kept my legs tightly shut
though my best friend and travel companion did not.
I watched her leave with the setting sun
tumble back into bed as the morning rose again.
I laid out on Venice beaches in the waning rays of sun
in the shortest dresses I could find
and felt sure that I was dying.

I've always been a woman of faith, after all
eyes cast downward, looking for scraps of Scripture on the ground
finding all the Commandments to remember.
I saw it written
that a man who looks at a woman with lust
should remove both his eyes.
Far better to enter the kingdom of heaven and be unable to see
than watch your whole body cast down.

But they don't remove their eyes, do they? They don't.
I never saw them try
though that's all I do.
I try hard enough to loathe myself
because only shame makes me feel I'm doing right.

Though it occurred to me just the other day
do I not have eyes worth keeping too? My hazel eyes...
I could swear on the last rays of sun that I do.
And haven't I the same hands, feet, mouth, organs...
affections and deep, deep passions
though I tried to kill such parts of myself in European summers

but they survived
and the serpent inside me mocks me now
drawing my passions and desires lower, lower
debasing me further, and further.

And certainly I am subject to the same diseases
healed by the same means
though I know the spiritualists would not believe it
and they would tell me, the only sickness is in your mind
and leave the truth of your illness behind
but I...
I don't know I could do that.

And I've been cooled by the same Vancouver winters
shivered in glee as the snow rushed down bright white above my window
and I knew I wouldn't be able to leave my house for a week.
And certainly I am warmed by the same summers too
sweltering hot on French, Italian, Spanish beaches
the globe inside my mind dims and flickers
as the heat grows heavy, thoughtless
caressing, oppressing me.

You pricked me, and I bled
bled, bled, bled for days
weeks, hours, months...
a year
longer, if I am honest.
I could have bled into the earth, as the spiritualists told me to
though I didn't feel I was up to leaving my bedroom.

You poisoned me, and I thought I died
though now I see my death was only a trick of the light
for the poison seeped into my veins, and made me effervescent
and you lit me on fire then
bright and cruel against a dark, unforgiving sky.

You wronged me, and *I had*—
see, and you told me that I didn't actually, just smile and take out my
    eyes, that was what you told me—
but you did wrong me.
You wronged me, and I'm sorry
but I had
I had to strike back
and harder, too.
You tell me I'm wrong
but I had to.

Daisy Bassen
Plimoth, during the next wave of plague

Pretending to be a colonizer forty hours a week
Isn't a bad gig: you get a name, a real one,
Unlike the adolescent sows, and a backstory
Instead of a date with the butcher to become
Spare-ribs and chops. No one is assigned
Dorothy Bradford grappling with melancholia
Or a future she never wanted, choosing
The water, lingering down among the cast-off
Clamshells, more present yet than all the men
And their statues—
                    None of the windows
Have panes, only shutters, so the only mask
You need is your character, your insistence
You don't know what a protractor is
While you explain the quadrant, the steel point
In your mind the whole time you talk
About right angles, how your high school drama
Coach would say you're not inhabiting the role
Enough, colonizing the colonizer. Just adding
A syllable to the world question, quest-i-on,
And putting up with the bitch of worsted stockings.
Other places are hiring, bonuses abound, but the man
You are already died once and you're fond of him
Now and the view of the cove, blue blue blue
From the meeting-house's battlements, frames
Of film cut to the floor. They never fired once
On an enemy and what could they have accomplished
That pox didn't, the pigs in the street ready to turn, run
Feral? You tell yourself it's an electuary, the honey

Keeping it from spoiling, but you'll be damned
If you come back next year, tell yourself it wasn't
All a mistake, lie as you lie to the tourists, lie
Even when they don't ask you anything, wandering by.

M. Cole
An Ode to Poe: My Soul's Narration

The silvered trees from a distance stood like quiet sentinels in the fog. It came so quickly this late fall morning, this foreboding, cruel to bones, chilling spirit cracking fog.

I hated it because it came so quickly and so quietly without a warning.

But what could I expect, Being so close to the river and dawn had not yet broken? I walked the jumbled path from the paved country road.

I liked this spot, normally.

Out here I was away from everything, even distant farmhouses and the growing buzz of town. Lately it had seemed that this little town was getting to be more like a city every day.

That was just a well-earned curse upon it.

Out here, I was free. I would come, and I would walk, and would always refresh my soul. But today, my soul was wrapped in spirit chains in this ghostly fog.

This fog, like a petulant specter, held everything in a near frozen bondage. Icy fingers, unseen in the mist, were punishing the living: the trees, the bushes, the wildlife here about, and even this poor human.

But still, there was an uneasy grace about this fog. It was unbidden and unwelcome, but did not capture anything in its path out of purposeful malice.

Unlike some ghosts, it had no specific hatred for the living. It simply was.

As I labored closer, careful with my steps in the darkened underbrush that spread across the frozen path, I could see the trees a bit more clearly.

They were as cold as I was, but still bid me welcome even though they dare not speak with their normal wind swept voice.

I stopped and came to realize that this fog was also doing me a kindness.

It may have been hiding the trail but it was also hiding me from the world. With such hiddenness, I could still rest and heal my weary soul.

Even an icy fog can give a gift.

Peter Urkowitz
Ten Miles Up the Trail

I didn't come here to sell you anything
If you want something, I want to show you where it is hidden
If you forget and come back tomorrow
I will hide it again

Offer me all your gold for my treasure map
I'll toss it out the window of our moving train
I was born in the caboose
And I'll die in the engine

Come up to the lodge
Show the boys your brush collection
They can smell your bootblack
Ten miles up the trail

Soap up your washboard
Really scrub those old philosophies
The stains will wash right out
But a musty smell still lingers
No matter what you do

Tiara Dinevska-McGuire
Kutlesh

Some suns crack the mountain
Into nothing, burned
Fragments of memory written nowhere
But on the backs of rotted teeth.
To the east, we are someone else,
To the south, we are no one at all, and
To the west, somehow, less.

Our sun, not permitted
To adorn manhole covers
Or church walls. I've thought about
Tucking it under my arm for safety.

My mother says
Your limbs will be tied to horses
To pull the sun away from you too.
To change your name too.

Chandra Rice
My Favorite Sin

salty and sweet,
her taut skin shines
with the effort of her arched back,
a pleasing pressure building as her heartbeat
    races
beneath lips kissed
                bruised and plump,
a name slipping sticky and rasping – a mantra
that hums
that sings
that crescendos
rippling through fingers hidden in sensitive flesh,
delightful and stirring and omnipotent,
until she succumbs
    spent
     exhausted,
loved into existence

Therapy

Almond eyes and flint in her fingertips:
I turn to ashes,
a grey mist rising from a dawn, hiding
the sun as she tries to bake the earth.
A sigh from her lips
quiets the storm,
reveals the iris petals,
pale and pink on her desk.
A gift.
Alive despite the surrounding darkness.
Prometheus and Phoenix.
Punished and redeemed.

Sister

Dark hair and dark eyes, living in dark places
but still effervescent
until your Tanqueray Polaris washed it away.
One sip, two sips, three bottles down.

Reached, grasped, lost your grip
to a bewitching lie veiled by the women at the cross
as they bowed to a rare mercy.

You battled in your dreams
for the life you wanted and the one you had,
for a truer north that lingered on your skin.
Your forgiveness is growing every day.

Kevin Brennan
Childhood Home

I see the place in dreams now, but distorted
with M. C. Escher dimensions and
paradox corners, the six of us playing
hide and seek with each other like lightning.

As houses go it was small, each of us
bivouacked to individual pup tents, trying
like tragedy to avoid one another so as to
keep truth stuffed in our mouths.

Drifting through discernible doubts, we all
tried self-serving gambits and floundered for
validation among the dirty socks strewn
around the rooms, metaphors flying.

Yet when escape was possible, I was the
only one who flew, vain about my prospects
but slapping myself tender over the years
with guilt that I should have stayed.

But even so, the walls were close,
the loose boards too telling, and the world
smaller than the house we lived in, a
virtual prison within a prison. Now I know

memory to be a backward-flowing escalator,
soundtracked by mall musicians in silkwear
and lit from above by artificial lumens
casting everything in a sweet, inaccurate glow.

I am that unhappy being

I am that unhappy being,
waiting for yes, nursing
belief in preservation and
visionary hope, all through
the night.

I am that unhappy being
who picks fights with fate,
waits till morning to kiss
the feet of favor, and fancies
the game over all.

I am that unhappy being
in love with beauty and
cursing necessary darkness,
drawn always to lucky
laughingstance.

I am that unhappy being,
easy in my own skin but
powerless against phantoms,
gathering life and strength
from small morsels.

I am that unhappy being
who knows the ropes,
bans fears, bears the wait,
and apprehends the ends of
all journeys to be joyous.

Serena Jacob
Strawberry River

Two young lovers stranded in the middle of nowhere;
Nowhere is beautiful.
Truck broken down, they call a mechanic
and explore the land with no mountains.
Miss and Missus dive into an alive forest
Growing green bugs and blue leaves
"Don't go too far," Missus cries
to Miss, who hears a crackling creek
And sweeps a bush to find a hidden
River of fat and small, dimpled and ripe
no-stemmed strawberries
Flowing from beginning to far-end.
Miss drops to her knees and
captures a bright red rushing strawberry to her
mouth
Missus cries - poison!
No, Miss groans, parting river with teeth
sinking into lush flesh again and again.
Missus, unable, forces her tongue into Miss' mouth
and bites into a juicy,
Explosive berry.
The lovers' skin turns pink. Miss cries
and their bodies
Dip like the bit at the top,
Fit like freckled and sticky ridges,
Juice staining, leaking sweetly,
Later, the pink fades,
One drags the other away, to the road;

Their truck gone, the day gone, their clothes flying away
Miss and Missus ran back to Strawberry River,
the horizon zion,
Current rush, eternal river fruit.

Anna Wright
Cigarette Pantoum

I knocked on my Aunt's door; "Who's this beautiful girl?"
She sets down her cigarette as if she'd never smoke again,
lifts her head towards the sky, and blows the smoke above my head.
She tells me I have the most beautiful legs.

She finishes her cigarette before saying she'd never smoke again.
Sitting upright on the couch she looks at me confused,
"How did you get such beautiful legs?"
She grins revealing her browning teeth.

Lying on the couch she looks at me confused,
as if I was a familiar stranger sitting on her chair.
She gives a polite smile revealing her browning teeth,
lights the next cigarette and talks to my mom.

I am a stranger sitting on her chair,
in her hospital room, next to her bed.
She then asks for a pack of cigarettes from my mom,
who respectfully declines and holds her hand

One last time she asks me "Who's this beautiful girl?"

Shane Ingan
Getting serious

You do your best to get a grasp on things:
Hölderlin's poetry, trimming your own bangs,
pitching a trekking pole tent, the Ukraine situation, etc.
Action is difficult. That is, living
the idea into the real, into
the realm of dirt and blood and heat
and eyes and money, is difficult,
so you'd rather write about it.

But how?

I do believe things could be better,
more beautiful, more spirited, less
senseless, perhaps more tragic,
and I have a few ideas about Christ
& Capital & the lives we live...

Neighbor, fellow stranger, lady
behind me in the checkout line,
I would like to get to know you better.
We could talk about those things that truly
affect the lives of those who, like you & I,
live here, those who, including you & I,
suffer. We could make a go of it, see
what holy mess we might get ourselves into
in a game of red rover local politics...

Then again, I would very much also
like not to know and try such things.

Do you follow the NBA?
Do you enjoy the paintings of John Marin?
Southern gothic literature? Not my forte, but...
Anyway, y'all should come over sometime.
We'll have a beer and watch a game,
or drink scotch and talk shop,
or sip sweet tea and listen to the birds...

I might just spend the evening alone.
I've had a long day and am very tired.

I make myself a turkey sandwich
with mustard and pickles and spicy cheese.
Around 11 or so, feeling lonely,
I pop some kettlecorn, put on a movie
and scroll through my Twitter feed.

Looks like the situation in Ukraine
is getting serious...

Ruth Towne
Torricelli Apparatus

"…and this is the wonder that's keeping the stars apart"
– e. e. cummings, [i carry your heart with me(i carry it in]

I am lonely soon, I imagine you are too.
When we drive together you keep the radio
low to subdue the soundwaves, but we talk
anyway, supplementing the time lost away.

We linger though this is not the first or last
of our goodbyes, but the outer space of spatial
relationship. Later, your plane brings the dim sky
closer to itself, this slow rate over time. Absence

demands I fill your place, remains greedy
and unsatisfied. Consider outer space, a near
perfect vacuum in nature, so you say. Gaseous
pressure stages constellations, heavenly bodies

among waves of light. Stars parse darkness
before they score aircrafts' backs, bringing
some close, taking you far. You and I relate
to light and sound—both move in space as waves

or not at all, so our movement has its restrictions,
careful definition. Outer space validates our void
and vacant art. Our two bodies separate forget
touch, remember the fact of past pressure only.

I separate space, alternate distance and absence.
To remember is pressure unto itself. Light, sound
waves pass between us. A face onscreen, a voice
reaches me at lightspeed. My inner ear vibrates,

tries to find inside the sine waves your body,
strange search in the dark. Hot air from my long
breath reacts above where I cross your gravel
driveway, contracts, cools. I learned fast never

to look back to the doorway where last I saw you.
If I was lonely then, what now? I say, you mute
the radio so that I won't sing so loud. This truth
does not crush me, in the background, still

music plays. Sound has no echo in space,
touch demands two objects. I sense another
absence. In my chest, radio waves vibrate.
I drive away from you and sing. Our distance

makes a strange way to be alone, a stranger way
to love—gives us both one atom of air per cubic
meter and says to each, partake, partake. We break,
communing in halves, separate until our vacuum

collapses at last. This event horizon, a vast black
hole, consumes all, even waves of sound and light.
Nature hates a vacuum, surrenders itself to create
from nothing, something, longs to satisfy the void.

Leap

For M. G. and C. P.

Black water as always, but low
for September. Along the rocks
the shore retreats from the water,

now pollen bands like tree rings
display the age of drought. Stones
shine, broken glass. Under my feet,

a boulder radiates noonday heat,
poises me over pond, patient, waits
for me to leap. Minnows, clouds

in schools crowd the tops of trees
to the western shore. And I rock,
a boat tied loose to a dock, prepare

myself to launch at water. A breeze
against bare skin reminds me fall
approaches. Sunlight sails over water

behind the wind, beams on waves
so its sheen mirrors scales of a fish.
I will jump soon. I recall Wetstone

Pond, then, when I cannot jump I cry.
My father by my life vest casts me in,
his swift skipping stone. I fear fall

and fauna, crayfish floating to wire
traps. Once I jumped, but I have fallen
older, my soul swims against my body,

its mesh coils. Now who will seize me?
Who throws me in? Still above Davis
Pond, I see the public pool twelve-feet

deep, and the boulder, my headstone,
another rigid Dover Y diving board,
never gives. Take a breath. That dive

was years ago, that dive is every day.
So now life, timeless deep dive. I wait
to leap, ready to leap, leap—I rise

from the water. Eyes open to graffiti
on the boulder's side. At eye-level
in red and white, a submarine.

James Kelly Quigley
Hot Cross Buns

It's a delightful torrid brilliant afternoon
the thin blue scar above the eastern slope
makes me heavy with hope and your remarkably
quick-witted silence is smog crawling a building

a sign says THIS GRASS NEEDS A BREAK the phrase
under the paving-stones, the beach arrests me
a merchant marine of robins takes no heed they keep
hoisting thick brown ropes of worm out of the surf

this snatch of lilies and their creamy trumpets
anywhere I go I'm liable to be recognized
the boy wonder whose heart was a macadamia nut
but that was decades ago and I've had operations

really I'm mostly like you except you are very cheeky
even as you sit there kinetic as the macaw
perched on a real tree sagging inside a polymer jungle
hot cross buns and coffee your treat and I'm grateful

admittedly I was getting a bit peckish and broody
fire engines so proud to be slick with drizzle
my ring in its particular shiny grime is smiling
the face of an aqueduct in a roster of taking-off birds

they have been here ever since birds were invented
murmuring and leaving behind shreds of pink silk
I'm all agog memorizing the way your sweat bursts
the dandelion shoots anticipate our footsteps

blowing their heads off to a song you wouldn't expect
tiny spirits with tiny white parasols are finally going home
and the unreachable island of pale yellow straw is
fucked in the ass with trash

Carolyn Kesterman
From the Space Between Songs

November's dawn sets the clouds above my tea ablaze
And highlights the copper buried in my hair.
There's a soft flavor to these mornings,
A soundless settling into the season as the
Sun peeks through fresh-bared branches to
Lend gentle warmth to a crisp, pale scene.
The roads nearby rush headlong from
Brilliant oranges and rich harvests to
Bold reds and taffeta bows,
But I want to linger here a little longer
In the quiet brown.

Across the street, a Cooper's hawk perches on a
Bough obscured a week ago.
Her catch is parting southward or burrowing in;
She doesn't seem to mind.
Her eyes point eastward,
Savoring the golden silence with me.
Maybe she's just resigned herself to the
Approaching dead of winter,
Or maybe she feels the reverberations of
Something low and steady
Rising from the shorn earth,
Sinking into the space between songs –
The deep inhalation before a new phrase begins,
The moment you pause and remember
What you're meant to say.

Margins

I've spent eight years trying to
Summarize the sweet grief
Of dried pine needles stuck
To the bare heels of my feet,
But prose doesn't linger on
Thick swatches of forest green.
It can't begin to scratch the
Surface of time lost in
Diagonal rows of light
Dashed across the
Afternoon floor.

I can't capture this collection of
Moments inside a louder plot,
One that reduces the smell of
Cantaloupe and coffee to
Scene development of Chapter Three,
That chains symbolism to the
Nebulous ties between
Mallard wings and tortoiseshell glasses,
Or casts foreshadows
Over napkins tied into
Mice at the kitchen table.

I see verses waiting in the
Folds of lace curtains and
Wish I were apt enough to
Honor them.
The places where I used to
Step back to summer are
Fading away.

They're painting over shutters and
Tearing down the walls you
Used to watch me climb.
But I can close my eyes and

Picture you there.
I can cut loose the plot to
Find you in the poetry.

Christian Cacibauda
Staircase Wit
for Matthew D'Occhio

From the French esprit d'escalier *(noun): A witty remark thought of too late, on the way home. Coined by French encyclopedist Denis Diderot.*

We were arguing fitness—how to train
with a barbell, how much protein you need
when you puffed up your chest and proclaimed:
Nothing worth doing is easy, and I, so entranced
by that locker-room logic, agreed. Till a glance
at my life (or any worth living)
showed me how full of shit that sentiment is.

Nothing worth doing is easy? That would mean
every sunset I've watched, every dream,
every broadcast and movie that I've *ever seen*—
all the reams of second-rate fiction I've read,
every trusting young novice I've lured into bed—
All a waste! *Life is hard, or should be, at least*

That's the credo of masochists, martyrs, and priests.
Nothing worth doing is easy. It's what God
said to Adam: *by the sweat of thy brow
shalt thou eat of the fields.* So it stands even now,
the Protestant Ethic and Catholic Guilt hold us still—
noses to grindstones and shouldering ploughs.

I would know. The love of hard work is a family curse.
Grampa Jack, for the sake of a new garden shed,
hauled his concrete by hand (though the wheelbarrow worked)
till the strain burst his heart and he keeled over dead.
Nothing worth doing is easy, he'd said.

And the sins of that father survived in my own,
who once, in a rage, smashed the family phone
(It wouldn't—or couldn't—place a long-distance call).
Nothing's simple, he grumbled, impatient and rankled
as he knelt with his tools, yellow paint, and white spackle,
and patched up the hole in the living room wall.

Of course, some things are hard. Nor would I—
a "privileged," white, suburbanite male—deny
that the battles hard-fought or the accolades won
by those whose ambitions loom larger than mine
have—and should have—their place in the sun.

But make no mistake: this sick mandate to prize
only that which comes hard is at worst self-abuse;
at best, self-deceit. That way madness lies,
and twelve-hour days at labors you loathe
just to pay for coarse meals, a roof, and rough clothes.

If that's what you want, why not barter
your life, with its first-world joys,
for the lot of another whose hardships hit harder?
Many do, and have done. Young Siddhartha
abandoned a kingdom. Saint Anthony, too.
Diogenes lived in a barrel. So can you.

Go and live among cynics, or sadhus, or saints.
Rejoice in their pain and their psalms.
Put to death all that's earthly within you.
Live on locusts, wild honey, and alms.

Nothing worth doing is easy, as we've struggled to learn.
If you still buy *that*, Spartan friend, let me tell you:
in exchange for the boons you've received—but not *earned*—
I've a lifetime of ashes and sackcloth to sell you.

Robin Gow
Leaves of Three

Bare-handed, my father and I unknowingly tore poison ivy
from necks of trees by the rectory.

His knuckles like plums. Knees, red-apples,
bitten by twigs and brush.

I was dying and I stood holding a pair of garden shears,
coming in to cut as my father pulled.

On my head I wore a veil. Did not try to push
the lace from my eyes. We destroyed collars of vine.

They say God is three: the father, the son, and the holy spirit.
So too comes poison. One leaf for every God.

My ribs; a bear-trap. There is so much
beneath body's surface. I ate holly leaves to survive.

As we worked my father complained how no one else
would come to clear away this side of the church grounds.

To be a martyr, you must first assume you are, in some sense,
only one. Killing poison was easy enough.

Once we tore it free, we dosed it in herbicide.
Watched as already leaves began to brown.

It was sweltering July. A time for redemption.
The next morning, we woke up with writhing fingers.

Our hands peeled and itched. My father showed me
how to rub lotion on. Only once he admitted,

"We should have worn gloves."
I lay in bed with my palms up after a shower. Hair wet

against my pillow. There, I dreamed
I was a church yard tree. Begged ivy to come.

Envelop my hands. Find the thirds of me
or else, find the whole to hold onto.

Igor Kojadinović
The Divine Madness

The days bond over a heavy rain.
At first light, I stare at the citrus tree outside my
window, dark brown and saturated. Two grapefruit the
size of melons weigh upon the branch, pushing one
another toward the earth. I shut my eyes for a moment and
imagine myself as the space between them until I remember
the bit of bread I've left on the counter to go stale.
I put on yesterday's clothes and notice the familiar
smell. Walking through the dining room I see myself obscured
in the faint gleam of hardwood. My umbrella leans against
a dim corner by the front door— its joints have begun
to rust from a lack of attention though it still repels water.
I lock the door on my way out and the first few drops
of rain tap hollowly on my canopy. The bread is coarse
under my arm and the world grey with dark clouds.
There is a lake a short walk away with trout and ducks
and large rocks I stood on as a boy. I stand along the bank
crumbling a bit of bread in my hand as a small brown
duck swims toward me bringing the whole lake with her.
The rain has been heavy for some days and the ground
is soft beneath me. Her small webbed feet
meet the ground and she walks toward me. I take
to one knee in the mud with my hand outstretched
and she takes the bread, nibbling politely at my skin.

Lawrence Bridges
Life of Hours

The street that likens red-faced tomatoes
to chimes, that cascades the gushing flow downhill
of similarities and stop signs, becomes my day
and life for a day, or a life of hours. Jumbled
pencils in a plastic bag, night wind still shivering
by morning, I announce my commencement -
a beginning not an end, in ticks and gentle
cracks of house wood and mind words
and a spell on the day to save each sound.
I'm nowhere in a forgotten legacy of time
you greet as it rolls down your street in rain,
invisible gust, or drying sunlight, whispering
nothing by saying the names of colored sounds.

Skylar Hendler
Morning Sun

My eyes squint at the morning sun,
my hair tied back in a little bun.

No warmth of an arm around my waist,
no one to kiss with my morning breath distaste.
No giggles while smothering you in tickles,
reality sinks in of a bed sheet to myself
filled with your riddles.

I can't feel your heartbeat so close to mine
that it follows in sync,
Because everything disappeared in the
brisk of a blink.

My nose wakes up stuffy from the morning sun,
only now without the scent of a newly loved one.

Dead Flowers

An internal electric shock every time someone has your hair,
sometimes people are shots instead of cups
and it's not really fair.

Time isn't what heals,
distraction is the real deal.
But that's not what I want,
that's if I'm being upfront.

We're all a lost cause,
looking for someone to make time pause.
I really thought I found my remote,
but here I am instead—
writing this meaningless note.

I don't mean to sit here and gloom,
but it's you that left me with dead flowers
I once thought would bloom.

Aaron Nobes
Uncorked

Floating motionless atop the Australian Mainstream.
Pirate amongst European carp and herpes virus.
Awaiting inspiration's ascent from bottom-fed dream
and partaking of hazy silt dredged from beers two-through-six.
Kicking back sans government kick-backs or sufficient kicks.
Stayed between locks monopolising flow during crisis.
Reflection grimacing in surface glimmering demure.
Angling for leviathan with far inadequate lure.

Shanna Williams
yuba river

at the end of the summer
we swam like we could breathe water
the sunscreen oiled around me like a
halo circling my skin
i drank it, i spit it out
i climbed until i couldn't feel my feet
on the hot rocks
crawling over the streams
passing water spiders and flecks of gold

we sat still
digging our hands into sand
bits and pieces
poking underneath our fingernails
we floated on top
with the salt lifting our bodies so high
the sun licking my skin
burning my eyelids
in a sweet way

at the end of the summer
i had 4 splinters in my feet and 6 cuts on my hands
my hair was split and dry
my skin freckled like a poppyseed bagel
fresh
i jumped off the big rock
falling until the water turned black and cold
i felt the fish on my flesh
it was freeing and it was hot and
i was not as sad
as before

Raymond Berthelot
A Long Way from Home

I pass two cowboys
standing next to their truck
on the side of the road, hood up
dust, grime
I do not stop.

I have a long way to go
and there is nothing,
I mean nothing
but fence, land, mountains
and the distance.

A dot moving on a very long, straight line
Only more land,
between here and there.

It sucks for them
but I drive on
somewhere between here and there
and offer a small prayer.

May help find its way
towards two rough cowboys
a broken truck
on the side of the road
a long
very long
road.

Street Light

One street light
yellow like the lollipop
in your hand
while sitting on the park bench
sunflower summer dress
cool in the heat of pigeons
looking for something something
anything to satiate this eternal hunger
that we all share
day after long day
by the light of the lamp
that turns us towards the morrow
and I must go now
really, I must go
bye now
bye

Sunset

Unless we can measure the distance
between heartbeats
time stands still
and the sun halts just above the horizon
indefinitely.

I hear the symphony
suspended in the mist
of a thousand waves
and I imagine
the patience of silence.

Between heartbeats
you and I float
in an open boat without paddles
on an ocean of memory

In measured rhymes
towards the consolation
of a single sun
suspended in amber
that refuses to set.

Kyra Trumbull
These gilded streets

i hate the feeling of listlessness
as if wandering in an abyss
of myself and my
solitude

Trapped in my own declaration
of procrastination
and the pressure grown
of this damn capitalist
society.

Demanding the slit wrist
of those useless scumbags
Decorating the streets and denying this skit
Homeless, unemployed, impoverished, *unproductive*

Hoping for help and receiving
a christening of
Disgust and disapproval
From princesses and mistresses
And men

Cold-blooded

Sometimes I wish
for the fortitude of a salamander.

Expelling noxious fumes while
slinking through the oleander,
and sunning on radiation graced rocks
unfettered from the need to pander
at the feet of some slanderous demander.

I'd like to dive below the water line,
catch sight of Aquarius as I take a gander

and find a silent sort of candor.

Amanda Dettmann
Dog Euthanasia

here are the ashes of my mother's hands. wear them
   as daring barrettes. mercy hair. like god grilling
     on easter. can hands be womb-less
if they've delivered countless babies? mewling ones
   with deformed paws. tails bent like birdbaths
     after baptism. her car littered
with anesthetic needles. kids joking about heroin.
   add an e and you don't get the women
     in my family. we slide through the hips
of the dead story. laughing. throw cinnamon over
   our shoulders like incense. here in this attic.
     raspberry stains on my thumbs. she knows
what I would have killed to never watch her. she practices
   departure well. who do I break for her.

Twenty-Fifth Birthday

A koi fish buries herself
      between the pond's

surface, her burbling backside
      a language hole. I want to be her

big spoon. Trust her
      destruction, all forms of intention,

like an orange making love
      to both her pulp & juice jive, pout

& bushy bramble. There is no cake
      for me here. Just an answer

crowd surfing its own
      question, my hands firecrackers

in a downpour, a koi leaping
      in defiant & ordinary stillness.

Amanda Dettmann

Annie Cook
Pilgrim

Sometimes the days are hard
bright things I must endure
to reach the heaven of
the nights
I stand before my window
lift the straps from off the skin
I keep hidden from the sun
for hours
I can lie still and quiet
not lie and say fine not
fear not death not still
stage four
Hours I can watch
moonlight on the water
hear teen voices on the road
feel the straps I let fall
as I step into the sea.

Dépaysement

I say the wrong word again
and my children correct me.
Do they worry, I wonder?
Do they wonder where I've gone?
I remember my grandfather
not long before he died
going for his walk
as always.

I went with him that day
April in New England
forsythia firing blooms
over walls of secret gardens.

He was a native son
of native sons of this city
all the way back
to when there were no
walls, no bricked off gardens.

Which is to say
he was no native,
no more than I.
Is that why, I wonder,
he lost his way?

He pointed at a grand house
no grander than his own.
I almost bought that,
he said, after the war.

But later my mother
told me he didn't.

Cheyenne Hicks
Audio Recordings

A throaty resonance of words to remember
ideas long ago thought, the voice sounds like a different timbre

Starters of stories and poetry in free verse
unfinished and unfiltered, left to freedoms of the universe

The writer, the speaker, the reader and listener
as one. Omnipresent, who will christen the recording
    -        *Delete*

Anniversary

Let us pretend this is an ode to you
to us. To all that we have become.

A lesson in thankfulness, a note of gratitude

For never making me feel
like calibrating or conforming
to fitting, a custom-made suit
just for you

Somehow a magnet, we were drawn together
in all my awkward imperfections
and imperfect habits. My quiet need to be alone, be with just me.
A pull of one opposite drawn to another
A forcefield joined by:in differences.

A lethal combination.

    Combustion!

Alex Stanley
Ruin, *Peñasco Blanco*

I stand in ruin with the ceiling beneath my feet,
inside shale the wind and rain made into steps,
among battered doorways and left behind places,
shards of pottery offer remnant beauty.
I stand in ruin and it stands for me,
ancient and hallowed rising up,
for the woman who made this patterned jug,
to hold what gives life when life didn't
keep her in its lofty arms. Gods bat their teeth,
ancestors grimace for what they've left behind,
untouched with the pain of leaving,
always in search of an offering for new life.

Ruin, *Sand Canyon*

The stones sing of the great mountains
beyond this abandoned village,
beyond the safety of the spring walls
and hummingbirds throttling into bloom.
I climb to find the gods playing in the runoff,
out of the stream, a woman dressed in white,
bearing corn, tells how this kiva fell into piles
of rock, before the piñon grew through its cracks.

Caroline Laganas
Pears

I.

You used to be in love with a boy who had a pear tree
        in his backyard. He put his hand over yours the day

he showed you how to pick fruit. Together, you held
        pears. Your wrists tilted horizontally. Skin sugared

by August heat. He said ready fruit would
        let go. Ripeness surrendered into your hands.

II.

My great-grandfather learned how to garden when
        he was a boy growing up in Italy. He brought everything

he knew to American soil. Dug for traces of home.
        Discovered evocations in ivy. Tomato vines. Found

memories beneath fig, plum, apple, olive, cherry,
        and pear trees. He clenched broken branches of the past.

III.

Everyone remained inside during one of the worst
     hurricanes in Massachusetts' history. Everyone

except my great-grandfather. Instead, he gathered
     rope from the cellar. Tied himself to the trunk

of his pear tree. Determined
     to defend it. And he did.

IV.

I lost track of how many days I spent searching
     horizons. Talking to no one but myself. Found

more comfort crying in front of
     reflections than him. He never loved rain.

I never loved him
     enough to tie a single knot.

I let go and blue skies surrendered into my hands.

Nick Maurer
Tender Embassy

Mortgage means death-pledge.
I called to tell you love means waiting in the dark.
Your overworn tires creep down our alley
like the gargoyles of Notre Dame at night.
Many nights you land your dart on the bullseye of meaning.
Many darts have yet to reach my tiny, ambulatory desk.
Wheels turn back from the sun's rationalizations.
Your face moves back and forth
like the brooms and dustbins of faith.
Desire stuffs the mind into the mouth.
Time worms it out. Plumes of exhaust,
so many of them out on the road
under the mild sun, under the weight
of a darkness we will never own.

D. E. Kern
Primrose Vale (for Michael J. Miller)

The spark appears in a notch,
or groove, between two hills
aspiring to the title mountain,
and extends like a burnished
thread of gunpowder marking
the way to an explosion—this
full-blown day with the power

to cast spells in shadows upon
the rock faces on the opposite
side of the valley. And I look
once more in the space between
where I often find you carving
a decisive path to cover distances
separating fixed points of interest,

pausing over clumps of beavertail,
your hat a tracking beacon as you
slip from one form of shade
to another—ocotillo or a saguaro
damaged by careless off-roaders
you wish were never here—
flattening sprays of primrose

blanketing this vale like a child
reluctant to leave their bed. But
seasons are sure to be different
this year. I see that as early as
October when I finally emerge
from my hydrocarbon vault just
to hear the wind carry the voices

of all my dead. They chatter
in the background of a baseball
broadcast drifting down the hall
from my office and convince me
to slip off to the machines for two
bags of chips—one for me and
my uncle who is salty and sweet

at the same time in a fashion that
now feels—not so vaguely—like
looking in a mirror. Then I make
a cup of coffee for my dad who
drinks the stuff nearly any time
of day—slurping a bit too loudly.
From her reclining throne, mom

holds court, balancing the tension
between our fear and admiration
on the tips of crochet needles she
clicks faster than the legs of Shane
Victorino—the Flyin' Hawaiian—
going first to third on a single.
I entertain them all tonight beside

the first fire of a new season while
searching the skies for Greek
archetypes and capital satellites
spinning in reverse across this
cyclorama where I catch a glimpse
of my college pal in pre-cancer days
firing a baseball past to my lost youth.

I toss a length of juniper on the blaze
and watch it burn from both ends then

mutter something about how Nihilists
cannot seem to outrun metaphors when
you—who is already oddly comfortable
with these ghosts—scold me for not
noticing flames are splendid dancers.

Felice Arenas
They Say

you may be
wounded, the wound, well
rounded, masterful, monkey-like
on a mattress, eternal
as a mother, smothering, marching,
choked, defaulting on credit, bolting
with the credit, glossy,
disruptively sad, copulating,
sad & copulating, hairless, a fabulist,
poor, worth
a lipstick, random, promised
but sacrificing, cranked, crumbling,
annexing glass, scandalous in silks
& drenched in jenever, sentimental,
wretched, wretched & yet with good
intentions (like Kafka wrote),
a murderer or tender
as a tick, a patron
of the arts, the art, anathema,
anamorphic, found,
frank, freshly cut
up with envy, walking bedlam
bleeding between your legs,
a tigress, goddess, vis-à-vis
God, wondering if God is They,
but you better look
good doing it, They say
to the girls.

Thaddeus Rutkowski
A Moment

I see a moment of happiness on my wife's face.
She smiles after she gets out of the bay water
before she sees I'm looking.
She holds a towel to her cheek
and stands over the bedsheet
we've brought to the beach.
We turned down the offer of reclining chairs,
at high prices, and even more
for the ones with sunshades.

She is glad to be where we are,
to be doing what we are doing,
which isn't much, really.
But we don't have to do anything more.
We are sitting on our bedsheet
next to each other on this small beach
around a living Atlantic reef
among the cruise passengers on their rented chairs.
We can stay as long as we want, for free.

Marcia Hurlow
Canoeing on Lake Olathe, September

—for my husband

The heron scoops up the thick air
with its blue wings, blue air
above and below, then over
the marsh and cattails, over
the orange glare of sun setting
faster and the cold settling
on my arms and face, your face
following the heron, your face
carved with grey bristles, silver
in the dusk and the lake silver
in the shadow of the heron
landing in her nest of herons,
night joining them, their secret
space, their safety, kept secret.

In the Flint Hills

—1 Thessalonians 5:16

The hackberry tree stands bent, limbs
splayed north, off balance in still air.

Its roots hold fast to limestone plates, bore
through crevices, burrow for water.

Anna's shoulders are bent and grooved
from her long march through tallgrass

to the spring for today's water, back
by dawn and prayer at the table.

Her hands grip together in a rock
of gnarled bones, tighter as the sun

rises, as the wind starts to blow.

Elizabeth Schmermund
Five Fingered Breathing

How my blood runs through
his veins, not just the angling
of his eyes or an affinity for myopia
but in the way he gasps at night,
asthmatic, yes, but spiraling
down all the permutations
of fear that he can
calculate and hold within;
the possibilities for pain that his
little body covers like an
overhung umbrella.

I taught him to trace
five small fingers with another,
to breathe in and out as his
pointer rises and falls,
but I never taught him
the panic that I bred
within him. I never taught
him how my body hums
tight like a cello string
or that I was born waiting
for the other shoe to drop,
for the punishment to begin.
I never taught him his
fearful inheritance.

Linds Sanders
Rattle

I grew up in sagebrush
and rattlesnake country.
Though, I've never seen one:
a rattlesnake.

When I was 8, a boy
in my class was bit
at his birthday party
and rescued.

My friend who I call sister
watches for them
curling around fence posts
on her family farm.

A man I know
cuts their heads off and
lines their ropy bodies up
for pictures.

I find that sad,
don't you?

Not everything
has the courtesy
to rattle.

Two technicians
with an ultrasound machine

can't make
heads or tails
of the lumps
under my husband's arm.

They tell him
to re-schedule
with new technicians
and stronger machines.

It's probably nothing.

Don't lymph nodes swell
all of the time?

Isn't it true
we don't always know
what the body does
and why it does it?

Still, if I could
root around
in his beautiful body
and wrench out
something monstrous
and squirmy--

I wouldn't hesitate
to heave a sharp shovel
down upon
its neck.

Aritrika Chowdhury
River of Dawn

You too move like the moon,
like sleep jutted out of its circle
taking after slick ballet steps.
Both of you elude me,
cast a djinn-like alcoholic stupor.
The lines of your face
stand in contrast to the moon,
though both of you haunt me with
the night ending -
a whole year of restless verses
and moon worshipping.

You mutter *aubade*
as I am terrorised by moving frames
Aubade brushes my hair
The moon slowly erases away.

Serious love-making has its consequences.
I can't sit still on the toilet seat
oblivious to the fainting moon.
She asks for respite like an urchin
with woe painted all over her,
She becomes a refugee and drenches
my then soporific existence
into a well of pity.
On her way out
she sprinkles confetti of concern.
She does it before the sun can eat them up.

I eat the first light
of aubade, as you said in bed.
I leave the sunlit sink sweltering,
How will the moon look tonight?

Aritrika Chowdhury

4 AM

Trumpeters of yellow light
will soon close in
with the muezzin's last cry
You finish your moonset song,
Newspaper men wake up early here
you remind me again
as the last syllables are caught midair
by the thud on your porch .
Ripe weekend eyes hardly consumed
the Saturday nutrients kept aside
We have come far from summer loos
and reflective car bonnets
Now the solstice carries a legacy of rituals.
An unofficial day of observation
Of stretched grief.
Of restricted breathing spaces.

I tear myself away from invites
to sleep over the Sunday morning
My blue porch has become a prayer rug for my cat
with a half- asleep paw on a faded ping pong.
She fills the blank of a companion.
When June turns into a tormentor
I come back home to her, sulking
for an uneventful dinner last night
She squints right at my encumbered chest
and tries hard to be unbothered
Striding and walking away like angry mothers
Angry loving mothers with their 'I told you so'
Yet remaining true to her kind
She permits me one night of indulgence
For a year long detachment.

Alejandra Hernández
Blue Dream

Hi
turn around n touch the
sky
don t know why but you re so
nice
neon vibes and funky
ties
don t nobody move that
tight
blue dream come like calming
ride
citrus oils to shine the
thighs
drink that thing you love so
fine
mind to keep your convos
light
lost feeling times be all
right
high risk come with rising
tides

Candice Phelan
Genesis of Rain

On the first day, there was rain. And it was used to mask the pain of all that came before. Something always comes before. Erased by time or shame or loss or victory. But on your first day, you existed in rain that poured down heavily and pooled around your bare feet and bare mind. You knew nothing from this so-called before that left behind stone ruins that couldn't be replicated. You are small but not weak. You know little but your body knows everything it needs to know about everything, not manufactured.

And you feel most things happen without permission. Being manipulated or commanded into existence, into motion, around you. And you scribble your panic out and away from you. Things happen with or without you even when you are the center. Or so you thought.

But your bloodline was founded in greed and violence. That which you can never escape. And maybe the original sin, that you can never know. You will never be privy too; it is your innate curse. One that you will suffer through forever. Because things don't need permission to exist, and emotions are not logical. Cannot be made logical. Submission is not a natural reaction to that
which is around you.

You are hope. The future. Everything and nothing exists within thanks to a bloodline of history you don't know. Will never know. That gave you a biped system and organs that function without your permission and ones that don't function because they are no longer useful, and you don't understand what they were even supposed to be used for.

Here we cope with words

You are hope.
The future.
Everything and nothing exist within you.
Around you.
Is centered around you.
Thanks to a bloodline of history, you don't know.
Will never know.
A bloodline that gave you a biped system and organs that function
without your permission
and organs that don't function because they are no longer useful.
You don't understand
what they were even supposed to be used for in the first place.

Because, on the first day,
there was rain.
It was used to mask
all the pain that came before.
Something always comes before.
A before erased by time, shame, loss, or victory.

But on your first day,
you existed in rain
that poured down thickly and pooled around your bare feet
and bare mind.

You know nothing from this so-called before
that left behind concrete ruins that can't be replicated.
You are small but not weak.
You know little but your body knows everything it needs
about everything not manufactured.

This before clings to you.

You feel most things happen without permission.
The rain will fall, and the earth will spin,
and you will still be standing there with no shoes on,
processing.
As everything is being manipulated,
commanded, encoded,
into existence,
into motion,
around you.

And you scribble your panic out and away from you.
Using pens with unknown origins
made out of materials that are manufactured
in a way that probably is killing you this very second.
Because ignorance is bliss,
and enlightenment can be reversed and forgotten.
Still, you believe things happen with or without you
even when you are the center.

Emotions are not logical
and cannot be made logical.
Submission is not a natural reaction to that which is around you.
But pain is something that scizes your body
without your permission,
and no one has an answer or solution for you.
So, you wonder if you alone
hold.
Suffer because of.
Your bloodline's curse
that plagues your every waking moment and your dreams.

Your bloodline was founded in dragon greed and gluttonous violence.
Everything is to be collected and consumed by you.

You are the most important one here.
Everyone and everything else are beneath you.
And you can never escape this belief.

Maybe the original sin,
that you will never know
and will never be privy too,
is your innate curse.
One that you will suffer through forever.
Because there is nothing that needs permission to exist.
To take up space.
Not you,
not me,
not curses,
not hope,
and not the plain ceramic vase full of white flowers that sits on your
    bedside table.

Sheree La Puma
The Lord Is Near To The Brokenhearted
Psalm 34:18

I grieve for the families who have suffered an
unfathomable loss," the governor says on Twitter.
When asked about guns, she points to the clouds
before settling her eyes on a carrier pigeon.

"We need to be prepared for a water shortage."
I think of the river, Colorado, how it once flowed
freely across the border - like me trying to escape
a killing field. America is burying its children.

When the war breaks out my legs are immersed
in plastic, stones underfoot. Tap water warmed
then cooled rehydrates skin. I hear the steady
march of waves up the beach. Then Spanish, a

tone I do not understand until I'm shown the video.
Little car, old man, grey tank. Ukraine. Here, this
salon, we usually talk about the beach, the gulf, the
tourists in between. Although, we once whispered

about men, Federales racing towards city center, as
if it was unusual. The boys are hoarding guns again.
Like a dam devouring a lake on drought parched land,
thirst is a terrible thing. In our grief we notice the terns

mistaking them for seagulls. Graceful with rowing
wingbeats, they carry sadness in their breath. I hug
the girl sweeping remnants of hair into a dustbin.
We do not talk about death, just the absence of life.

CONTRIBUTORS

CONTRIBUTORS

FELICE ARENAS wrote Netflix synopses for a decade and covered cinema and music for *HuffPost* before earning her MFA from New York University, where she taught creative writing and was a Global Research Initiatives Fellow. She teaches editing at Berkeley. Her work has also appeared or is forthcoming in *Literary Hub*, *Harvard Review*, *The Georgia Review*, and more. Born and raised in Chicago, she has lived in Los Angeles, New York, Brooklyn, and Shanghai.

SARAH AZIZ is a poet, translator and artist based in Kolkata, India. She is currently majoring in English Literature at Loreto College, University of Calcutta. In 2021, her translation of Bangladeshi activist and author Pinaki Bhattacharya's *History of Bengal: from Ancient to British Rule* was published.

SIMON ANTON NIÑO DIEGO BAENA lives in the Philippines with his wife and child. He is the author of two chapbooks, *The Magnum Opus Persists in the Evening* (Jacar Press) and *The Lingering Wound* (2River). His work is forthcoming in *The Columbia Review*, *South Dakota Review*, *The Twelve Mile Review*, *Apalachee Review*, and elsewhere. He is a semi-finalist for the Tomaz Salamun Prize at VERSE (2021).

ANON BAISCH is currently a data analyst working in the semiconductor industry. Anon's poems have been published most recently in *Defunct*, *New Note Poetry*, *2River*, *The Write Launch*, and forthcoming in *Waxing & Waning*.

TOHM BAKELAS is a social worker in a psychiatric hospital. He was born in New Jersey, resides there, and will die there. He is the author of 21 chapbooks and several collections of poetry, including *The Ants Crawl In Circles* (Whiskey City Press, 2022). He runs Between Shadows Press.

ENNE BAKER is an American poet with Montenegrin lineage. His first and only poetry collection is *The White Colossus*.

JERRICE J. BAPTISTE is a poet and author of eight books. She has been published in *Mantis*; *The Yale Review*; *Kosmos Journal*; *The*

Tulane Review; Eco Theo Review; The Caribbean Writer and many others. Jerrice is Poet in Residence at The Prattsville Art Center in Prattsville NY. She is nominated as Best of The Net by *Blue Stem* in 2022. Jerrice joyfully teaches poetry where she lives.

DAISY BASSEN is a poet and community child psychiatrist who graduated from Princeton University's Creative Writing Program and completed her medical training at The University of Rochester and Brown. Her work has been published in *Salamander, McSweeney's, Smartish Pace, Crab Creek Review, Little Patuxent Review,* and *[PANK]* among other journals. She was the winner of the So to Speak 2019 Poetry Contest, the 2019 ILDS White Mice Contest, the 2020 Beullah Rose Poetry Prize, and the 2022 Erskine J Poetry Prize. Born and raised in New York, she lives in Rhode Island with her family.

JOHN PETER BECK is a professor in the labor education program at Michigan State University, where he co-directs Our Daily Work/ Our Daily Lives, a program that focuses on labor history and the culture of the workplace. His poetry has been published in a number of journals including *The Seattle Review, Another Chicago Magazine, The Louisville Review,* and *Passages North,* among others.

NATALIA BELTCHENKO is a poet and translator. Born in Kyiv, she is a recipient of the Hubert Burda Prize (Germany, 2000) and the National Writer's Union of Ukraine Mykola Ushakov Prize in Literature (Ukraine, 2006). Finalist of the Gennady Grigoriev Prize (Russia, 2013), the L. Vysheslavsky's "Poet's Planet" prize-winner (Ukraine, 2014). Her works include eight collections of poetry and numerous magazine selections and anthology publications, both in Ukraine and abroad (in English, German, French, Polish, Korean, Dutch, Bulgarian, etc.).

WILL BERRY is a writer & filmmaker from Maine. His short stories have received acclaim from *The Florida Review, The Pinch,* and *Zoetrope: All-Story.* His screenplays have been selected at Scriptapalooza, the Austin Film Festival, and PAGE, among others. A graduate of Brown, Will begins his MFA journey at the University of Alabama this fall.

RAYMOND BERTHELOT is the Historic Sites District Manager for the Louisiana Office of State Parks and also teaches at Baton Rouge Community College. His work has appeared in diverse publications such as *Peregrine Journal*, *Apricity Magazine*, *The Elevation Review*, *Journal of Caribbean Literatures*, the *Carolina Quarterly* and *DASH Literary Journal*. A chapbook of poems, *The Middle Ages*, is currently available with Finishing Line Press.

MAGGIE BOWYER (they/them/theirs) is a poet, cat parent, and the author of various poetry collections including *Ungodly* (2022) and *When I Bleed* (2021). They are an essayist with a focus on Endometriosis, chronic pain, and trauma. They have been featured in *Bourgeon Magazine*, *Capsule Stories*, *Plainsongs Poetry Magazine*, *The Abbey Review*, *Troublemaker Firestarter*, *Wishbone Words*, and more. They were the Editor-in-Chief of *The Lariat Newspaper*, a quarterfinalist in Brave New Voices 2016, and they were a Marilyn Miller Poet Laureate. You can find their work on Instagram and TikTok @ maggie.writes.

KEVIN BRENNAN is the author of eight novels, including *Parts Unknown* (William Morrow/HarperCollins), *Yesterday Road*, and, new in April 2023, *Three for a Girl*. His work has appeared or is forthcoming in *The Berkeley Fiction Review*, *Mid-American Review*, *Twin Pies*, *The Daily Drunk*, *Sledgehammer*, *Elevation Review*, *Tiny Molecules*, *Flash Boulevard*, *Fictive Dream*, *Atlas and Alice*, *LEON Literary Review*, *MoonPark Review*, *talking about strawberries all of the time*, *Atticus Review*, and others. A *Best Microfiction* 2022 nominee, he's also the editor of *The Disappointed Housewife*, a literary magazine for writers of offbeat and idiosyncratic fiction, poetry, and essays. Kevin lives with his wife in California's Sierra foothills.

LAWRENCE BRIDGES's poetry has appeared in *The New Yorker*, *Poetry*, and *The Tampa Review*. He has published three volumes of poetry: *Horses on Drums* (Red Hen Press, 2006), *Flip Days* (Red Hen Press, 2009), and *Brownwood* (Tupelo Press, 2016).

SKYLAR BROWN is a private English instructor. She has been passionate about writing and poetry for years, and has had a few pieces of work (both poems and short stories) published in various anthologies.

GARY BUNTING is originally from England but currently splits his time between England and New York. He is one of the writers at Hello America Stereo Cassette, which released his spoken word album *Northern Sketches* in 2021.

CHRISTIAN CACIBAUDA is an itinerant poet and writer. A Native of Reno, he was educated there at the University of Nevada, and at the Universidad del País Vasco, San Sebastián, Spain. His work has appeared in *Red Rock Review, Brushfire Literature & Arts Journal, West Trade Review,* and *Hive Avenue Literary Journal.* He lives in Beijing.

JENNA CARDINALE writes poems. The author of two chapbooks, her work can be found in *Allium, Verse Daily,* and *Pom Pom Press.* She lives in Brooklyn, New York, which is her favorite place.

M.P. CARVER is a poet and visual artist from Salem, MA. She is Director of the Massachusetts Poetry Festival and miCrO-Founder of the journal *Molecule: a tiny lit mag.* In 2022, her poem "You & God & I" won the New England Poetry Club's E.E. Cummings Prize. Her work has appeared in *9x5,* an anthology of emerging voices from Only Human Press. Her chapbook, *Selachimorpha,* was published by Incessant Pipe in 2015.

ARITRIKA CHOWDHURY is a student at Jadavpur University pursuing a master's degree course in Economics. For the tropical slow summers she has spent eating lunch and dinner in bed, and watching the sun go up every dawn with tired eyes, what kept her company like a caring grandmother is poetry. Poetry has been a saving grace and hence she writes. Her greatest inspiration is Sylvia Plath, with whom she claims to have a spiritual connection. Her work has appeared in the *Trouvaille Review, Gulmohur Quarterly* and *Saahitya Ekhaan* in Kolkata International Book Fair. She lives in the city of Kolkata, India.

M. COLE is a sixty-one year old lover of all things dark and mystical or mysterious. Otherwise, he has an upbeat outlook on life after two winning battles with leukemia. He believes beauty can be appreciated even in life's hardest moments.

ABIGAIL KIRBY CONKLIN is an educator and writer currently based in Toronto, Ontario. She is the author of the 2020 chapbook *Triage* (Duck Lake Books), the Substack "Recently," and a variety of other works that can be found in the *Tule Review, Sugar House Review, Elevation Review, Lampeter Review,* and *Wild Roof Journal.* She's online at abigailkirbyconklin.us and @akc_poetry_prints

ANNIE COOK lives in Providence, Rhode Island. Her work has appeared in *The Elevation Review* and *The Dillydoun Review*. She received a PhD in English Literature from the University of Wisconsin - Madison, where she also studied Creative Writing at the graduate level.

JANELLE CORDERO is an interdisciplinary artist and educator living in Spokane, WA. Her writing has been published in dozens of literary journals, including *Harpur Palate*, *Autofocus* and *Hobart*, while her paintings have been featured in venues throughout the Pacific Northwest. Janelle is the author of four books of poetry: *Impossible Years* (V.A. Press, 2022), *Many Types of Wildflowers* (V.A. Press, 2020), *Woke to Birds* (V.A. Press, 2019) and *Two Cups of Tomatoes* (P.W.P. Press, 2015). Stay connected with Janelle's work at www.janellecordero.com and follow her on Instagram @janelle_v_cordero.

SELDEN CUMMINGS is currently working toward my MFA in poetry at Columbia University, and recently has been published (or accepted for publication) by the *New Croton Review*, *86 Logic*, *Some Kind Of Opening*, *Chapter House Journal*, and *Matchbox Magazine*.

Based in the U.S. Pacific Northwest, ALLISON A. DEFREESE leads literary translation workshops for the Oregon Society of Translators and Interpreters. Her work appears in *Crazyhorse / swamp pink*, *Gulf Coast*, *Harvard Review*, and *New England Review*. Her translation of Carolina Esses's book *Winter Season* (*Temporada de invierno*) is forthcoming from Entre Ríos Books (Seattle) in 2023.

AMANDA DETTMANN is a queer poet, performer, and educator who is the author of *Untranslatable Honeyed Bruises*. She earned her MFA from New York University and has received support from the *Kenyon Review* Writers Workshop. Her work has been nominated for a Pushcart Prize by *The Emerson Review*, and she was one of two finalists for the *Action, Spectacle* contest judged by Mary Jo Bang. Dettmann's work has appeared or is forthcoming in *The Amistad*, *South Florida Poetry Journal*, *The Adroit Journal*, *The Oakland Review*, and *The National Poetry Quarterly*, among others.

TIARA DINEVSKA-MCGUIRE is a first-generation Macedonian-American poet and translator from Cleveland, Ohio. Her poetry can be read in *Poet Lore*, *The Common*, *Cagibi*, and elsewhere. In 2022 she received her MFA from Boston University, where she also was awarded a Robert Pinsky Global Fellowship and served as a Teaching Fellow. Currently, she is focused on further developing her abilities as a translator from Macedonian to English.

MEHMET KAAN EĞRETLI is a second grade English Literature from Turkey who has been greatly influenced by Wilfred Owen contextually and Gerard Manley Hoppkins considering literary style.

MIHAI EMINESCU is often regarded as Europe's last great Romantic writer, though some critics prefer to focus on the pre-modernist chords of his poetry. Born in 1850 in Moldova, he studied in the Germano-Romanian cultural centre of Cernauti (now Chernovtsy, Ukraine), Vienna and Berlin, where he was influenced by Schopenhauer's philosophy, Western literature and German translations of ancient Indian texts. Most of his literary work came to a halt in 1883, when he suffered the onset of a mental illness that led to his death in 1889 in an asylum in Bucharest, Romania. Eminescu modernised and transformed Romanian literature profoundly.

Writer and journalist CAROLINA ESSES was born in Buenos Aires and lives in Bariloche (Argentina). She has published several books including *Versiones del paraíso/Variations on Paradise* (Del Dock, 2016), *Temporada de invierno/Winter Season* (Bajo la luna, 2009, translation by Allison A. deFreese forthcoming by Entre Ríos Books, Seattle, in late 2023). Her poems have previously been translated into French and have appeared in the anthology *Poésie récente d'Argentine, une anthologie possible/Recent Poetry from Argentina: a Possible Anthology*, published by Editorial Reflet de Lettres. She is also author of several novels and has been literary critic for *La Nación*, Argentina's leading daily paper, for many years.

NATALIE FAINSTEIN has an MFA in Theatre Arts from Tel-Aviv University. Since her graduation, she has taken part as an actress in a variety of theatre shows directed by Israel's most prominent directors. She has expended her fields of expertise "in all things drama" by perusing additional careers in teaching, translating and writing. Natalie is also a voice-over artist with her own home recording studio, specializing in book narration. She is delighted and constantly challenged by Prof. Gad Kaynar's poetry and considers it a great honor to be the English translator of his poems.

MICHAEL FAVALA GOLDMAN is a translator of Danish

literature, a poet, educator, and jazz clarinetist. He has translated 16 books of Danish poetry and prose, including Dependency, book three of *The Copenhagen Trilogy* by Tove Ditlev*sen*, which was selected among *New York Times'* Ten Best Books of 2021. His third book of poetry, *Small Sovereign* was awarded First Prize for Poetry in the 2022 LA Book Festival. He lives in Northampton, MA, where he has been running bi-monthly poetry critique groups since 2018

KAZUYO FUKAO is a sake maker residing in Gujo, Japan. She spends her days working as a brewer and learning the traditional work and celebration songs and poetry of the region. Inspired by a wood barrel brewed sake made the traditional way, she wanted to learn how to make sake just as people had done before the advent of stainless-steel tanks. Now, in addition to making the sake, she is apprenticing with the only remaining boatwright in the prefecture, and training to make the wooden barrels, starting with cutting down the bamboo used as the ties for the cedar planks.

Danish author, musician, painter, and sculptor ROLF GJEDSTED (1947-2022) wrote fifty-five works of poetry, fiction, translation, and non-fiction. Gjedsted never achieved great notoriety as a writer during his lifetime, but his poetry reveals his dedication to musicality and the transformative power of language. Also a black belt and karate instructor, Gjedsted was fearless in penetrating the substance of whatever topic he approached.

AMELIA GLASER is Associate Professor of Russian and Comparative Literature at U.C. San Diego. She is the author of *Jews and Ukrainians in Russia's Literary Borderlands* (2012) and *Songs in Dark Times: Yiddish Poetry of Struggle from Scottsboro to Palestine* (2020). She is currently a fellow at the Radcliffe Institute for Advanced Study.

HRISHIKESH GOSWAMI is a Contemporary Naturalistic poet from Assam, India who specializes in writing about nature and realism coalescing fiction and non -fiction in a sophisticated blend. Hrishikesh's poems have been critically analysed by *Fruit Journal Manchester* (UK), *Acorn (A journal of contemporary haiku)*, *The Leading Edge Magazine*, *BreakBread Magazine* and has been published by *The Assam Tribune, Blue Lake Review, Indian Poetry Review, NEZINE, Noverse Foundation and FoxGales Publishers, Poem hunter-The World's*

Poetry Archive, the *Weaver Magazine*, *Poets India*, *Soul Connection* brought up by Guwahati Grand Poetry Festival, *Anthology Still I Rise* brought out by Wingless Dreamer, *Winter Poems Anthology* brought out by Poets Choice, *Cultural Reverence* and many more.

ROBIN GOW is a trans poet and young adult author from rural Pennsylvania. They are the author of several poetry books, an essay collection, and a YA novel in verse, *A Million Quiet Revolutions* (FSG Books for Young Readers, 2022). Gow's poetry has recently been published in *POETRY*, *Southampton Review*, *Poet Lore*, and *Yemassee*.

MUYAKA BIN HAJI AL-GHASSANIY (1776 – 1840) was the earliest secular Swahili poet whose identity is known. He has been credited with bringing Swahili verse "out of the mosque and into the marketplace" with his commentary on daily life in Mombasa and its frequent battles defending its independence against the Omani Empire. He also popularized the mashairi quatrain form that serves to this day as the predominant form of Swahili verse.

SEIJI HAKUI (b. 1986) is a Japanese poet living in Tokyo. His debut collection of poems, *Sonnets and Translations*, composed entirely in Classical Japanese, was published in 2022 by Shichosha.

NANCY HAMILTON is a writer, translator, and researcher in Stanford, CA. She completed her MA degree in East Asian Studies at Stanford University, focusing on Japanese literature and poetry. She is a practitioner and instructor of Chanoyu and is currently researching a project on the poetic impulse of Tea Practice.

In print, VICKY MACDONALD HARRIS's poems reside in the *NaPoChapBook* and *The Lincoln Underground*. Her poem, "Disaster Capitalism," was published in *The Flat Water Stirs: An Anthology of Emerging Nebraska Poets* in 2017. Online her poems can be found at *Tiny Poems*, *Two Cities Review*, *Poets and Artists*, *Hobble Creek Review*, *the24project*, *The Prairie Sage*, and in Women Poets Wearing Sweatpants Tumblr. Recent work in *Fiery Scribe Review*, *Janus Literary*, *Strange Horizons*, *Ellipsis Zine 12*, and *Great Lakes Review*. Forthcoming essay in *Whale Road Review*.

SKYLAR HENDLER (she/her/hers) is a senior at the University of Florida majoring in Criminology and philosophy on the pre-law track. In between fulfilling my obligation on law executive boards and mock trial team practices, Skylar writes poetry in her notes app to help cope with all the emotions that come with being a woman dating in college. She started songwriting when she was only a couple of years old but soon discovered poetry as another means of expression.

ALEJANDRA HERNÁNDEZ is a Latinx poet from San Diego, Ca. She is currently working on an MFA in Poetry from San Diego State University. She completed a Bachelors in Creative Writing from UC Riverside. This is the poet's first publication.

CHRISTOPHER HONEY is a candidate in the MFA program at the University of Saint Thomas. His poetry, essays, and articles have appeared in numerous publications, including the *Pomona Valley Review*, the *Building Trades News*, and *Montgomery Living Magazine*. He lives in Washington, DC with his wife and daughter.

LILY KAYLOR HONORÉ is a queer Californian poet, essayist, and MFA candidate at New York University, where she teaches in the undergraduate creative writing program. She is Fiction Editor of *Washington Square Review*. Her recent work can be read in *Foglifter* and *Through Lines Magazine*. Honoré lives in San Francisco and Brooklyn.

SARAH HORNER is a self-proclaimed poet, obsessive literature student, and shameless hedonist based in Minneapolis, Minnesota. Her writing explores themes of religion, femininity, mental illness, and the queer experience. When she doesn't have her nose in a book, you can probably find her romanticizing her life in her favorite art museum or campus library.

SOPHIE HOSS is currently pursuing a BFA in Creative Writing from Stony Brook University. Her work has been featured in *BOMB*, *The Los Angeles Review*, *Storm Cellar*, and elsewhere. She has attended workshops at the Southampton Writers Conference and the Iowa Writers Workshop.

MARCIA L. HURLOW's first full-length book of poems, *Anomie*, won the Edges Prize (WordTech). She also has five chapbooks. Her individual poems have appeared in *Poetry*, *Poetry Northwest*, *Chicago Review*, *Poetry East*, *Nimrod*, *River Styx*, *Zone 3*, *Baltimore Review*, *Cold Mountain* and *The Journal*, among others. She is co-editor of *Kansas City Voices*.

YULIYA ILCHUK is Assistant Professor of Slavic Languages and Literatures at Stanford University. She is the author of *Nikolai Gogol: Performing Hybrid Identity* (2021). She is currently researching memory and identity in post-Soviet Russian and Ukrainian literature.

SHANE INGAN is from Indiana and lives in Detroit. Their first book of poetry, *Lost Loves*, will be released early next year through Forsythia Press.

SERENA JACOB is an emerging writer from San Diego, CA. She enjoys surfing, reading and writing, and the mountainous side of nature.

OM PRAKASH JHA writes poems and fictions. His poems and short stories have appeared in many reputed journals including *The Indian Literature*, *The Daily Tribune*, and *Rigorous*. His poems have been selected by *The Elevation Review* and *The LKMNDS* podcast. He is the author of an inspiring book *Management Guru Lord Krishna*. He has a Doctorate degree in Translation Studies. He has also translated books of two Turkish writers: Ahmet Hamadi Tanpinar and Yekta Kopan. Email: opjha189@yahoo.com , twitter: @OP Jha17

KATERYNA KALYTKO is a poet, prose writer, and translator. She has published nine collections of poetry and books of short stories. She has received many literary awards and fellowships, among them the Central European Initiative Fellowship for Writers in Residence, KulturKontakt Austria, Reading Balkans, Vilenica Crystal Award, Joseph Conrad-Korzeniowski Literary Prize, BBC Book of the year and Women in Arts Award from UN Women. Striking imagery emerges in her recent poetry like puzzle pieces that create a violent and shocking picture of war, conveying the loss and pain that is experienced during a search for safety and identity amidst the war.

GAD KAYNAR-KISSINGER (73) is a retired Associate Professor from the Theater Department at Tel Aviv University. His poetry was published in major Israeli literary periodicals and supplements, and compiled in seven books, including a bi-lingual Hebrew-Spanish publication *Lo que queda* (*What Remains*). For ADHD he won "The General Israeli Writers' Union" Award (2010). Kaynar is a stage, TV and film actor, and translator of 70 plays from English, German, Norwegian and Swedish. For his Ibsen translations he was designated in 2009 by the Norwegian King as "Knight First Class of the Royal

Norwegian Order of Merit."

PITAMBER KAUSHIK is a writer, journalist, educator, poet, and independent researcher based out of Jharkhand, India. His writings have appeared in over 180 leading publications across 50+ countries. He has been recognised by the Limca Book of Records and has received podium finishes in multiple literary contests.

GABRIELĖ KEMĖŠYTĖ is a Lithuanian scholar of premodern Japanese literature. A graduate of Asian Studies (Japanology) program in Vilnius University, she works in both Lithuanian and English and specializes in classical waka poetry. Her current research focuses on readings, translation, and contextualisation of Fujiwara no Teika's lesser-known poetry collection *Hyakunin Shūka*.

D. E. KERN is a writer and educator from Bethlehem, PA. His work has appeared in *Appalachian Review, Glint, Limestone, Reed, Rio Grande Review* and the *Owen Wister Review*. He teaches at Arizona Western College where he directors the Honors Program.

CAROLYN KESTERMAN is a Cincinnati native whose poetry and fiction have appeared in seven publications, including Issue 64.2 of *The Poet's Touchstone*, Issue 10.1 of *Plumwood Mountain Journal*, and Issue 49 of *The Notre Dame Review*. She is currently finalizing her first novel and first chapbook.

ERIKA KIELSGARD is a writer, singer, and artist researching disruptive patterns for protective concealment in nature. Most recently, their work is in *Footprints: an anthology of new ecopoetry* (Broken Sleep Books, 2022), and has found generous homes in *Bone Bouquet, Cordella Magazine, Maudlin House, The Penn Review, Volume,* and others. She lives in Brooklyn, NY.

IGOR KOJADINOVIĆ is a Serbian poet. Born in Ljubljana, Slovenia, he relocated to the United States, where he has worked as a firefighter and paramedic for the last eight years. He currently attends The University of Central Florida and is pursuing studies in Philosophy. His work appears or is forthcoming in *Delmarva Review, The Write Launch,* and *Anamnesis Journal of Philosophy*.

CAROLINE LAGANAS earned an MFA in Creative Writing from California Institute of the Arts and a BA in Journalism from

Pepperdine University. Her work has been supported by the Bread Loaf Writers' Conference, *Kenyon Review* Writers Workshop, and Napa Valley Writers' Conference. She was an International Merit Award winner in the *Atlanta Review* 2022 International Poetry Competition. Her poems have appeared or are forthcoming in *Five Points*, *New Orleans Review*, *Poetry East*, and others. She is currently writing and illustrating her first book of poetry.

SHEREE LA PUMA is an award-winning writer whose work has appeared in *The Penn Review*, *Redivider*, *The Maine Review*, *Stand Magazine*, *Rust + Moth*, and *Catamaran Literary Reader*, among others. She earned her MFA in writing from CalArts. Her poetry has been nominated for Best of The Net and three Pushcarts. A reader for the *Orange Blossom Review*, her latest chapbook, *Broken: Do Not Use* is currently available at Main Street Rag Publishing.

KATHRYN LAURET lives in Colorado. She works with elementary school students with special needs.

KEVIN LEMASTER's poems have been found at *SheilaNaGig* online, *The Slipstream*, *Triggerfish Critical Review*, *Route 7 Review*, *West Trade Review* and others. He has work forthcoming in *Main Street Rag*. Kevin is the co-editor of the upcoming anthology *Poetry by Chance* and the judge of the Golden Die Contest that supplied the poems for the anthology. He is currently a Level 2 reader for Ariel Publications. His work in *Rubicon: Words and art inspired by Oscar Wildes De Profundis* was nominated for a Pushcart prize.

ASTER LEONIS is a graduate student at Stanford. They grew up in France and left at 18 to study abroad and explore the world.

PRIA LOUKA is a writer and translator of Greek poetry. A book of her translations of George Sarantaris' poetry, *Abyss and Song: Selected Poems*, is forthcoming with World Poetry Books (2023). She is the recipient of a Fulbright Fellowship that has allowed her to pursue her passion for modern Greek literature. She is the author of *The Courage to Walk and Write* (Alphabetics) and has published an extensive photographic essay on Greece. Louka, a graduate of Princeton University, currently lives in Thessaloniki, Greece.

BRANDON MARLO is a 26-year-old janitor from New York who has found personal freedom in his own fallibility. Holding a mirror to his habits, relationships and overall lifestyle in the name of growth. Though perhaps it's just to laugh at the sheer absurdity of it all, for his own sake.

BAZ MARTIN GIBBONS is author of *Beyond the Screenplay* and *Cinema and Its Discontents* (MacFarland). His essays on film have been published in *Directory of World Cinema* and *World Film Locations* published by Intellect Ltd. (UK) and University of Chicago Press (USA). His most recent publications include a chapter from his memoir *I Sing the Mind Electric* (*Watershed Review*) and translations of Brazilian poets Augusto dos Anjos and Murilo Mendes in *POETRY*, *Lunch Ticket*, *The Antonym*, and elsewhere. He currently divides his time between Brazil and England. He is the recipient of the 2023 Gabo Prize for Literary Translation.

NICK MAURER is a visual artist and writer who lives in Costa Mesa, CA. He received an MFA from UC Irvine.

NUPUR MASKARA is a freelance content writer in India. Her work received the Orange Flower Poetry Award in 2020. Nupur's work has been anthologized in *The Kali Project* and published in magazines like *Wry Times*, *Last Leaves*, *The Gateway Review*, *Rigorous*, *The Loch Raven Review* and *Zoetic Press*. She has authored two poetry books—*Insta Gita: With Arjuna's Perspective in Poetry* and *Insta Women: Dramatic Monologues by Drama Queens*. Nupur blogs at nutatut.com. Tweet to her @nuttynupur.

MURILO MENDES was born in Juiz de Fora, Brazil in 1901. In 1930 Mendes published his first collection, *Poemas: 1925—1929*. Mário de Andrade—the father of Brazilian modernism—celebrated the collection stating it was "historically the most important book of the year." In the 1950s, Mendes emigrated to Europe meeting surrealists André Breton, Franics Picabia, René Magritte et al. Surrealism was, and would remain, a significant feature of Mendes' mature work. Mendes settled for a time in Rome, teaching Brazilian literature, then retired to Lisbon where he died in 1975 two years after completing his final collection, *Retratos-relâmpago*.

Scottish writer, EMMA MOONEY believes passionately in giving everyone a voice. Her poetry this year has featured, or is upcoming in *The Poets' Republic*, *MockingOwl Roost*, *Dreich*, *Razur Cuts*, *Soor Ploom Press*, *Voices for the Silent*, *Dear Politicians* and *Poetry Scotland*.

Earlier this year Emma was honoured to be Makar o the Month for The Scots Language Centre, and she enjoys performing at live events across the central belt of Scotland where she lives. Emma was awarded a master's with distinction in Creative Writing from the University of Stirling. Check out her work at www.emmamooney.co.uk

ARIANA MOULTON is a 3rd grade teacher and writer living in Chicago with her two daughters and husband. She grew up in Cornwall, Vermont, attended Bates College and has her master's from Columbia College. She is inspired by nature, politics, Chicago, and the people and landscapes of Vermont. Her writing appears in *Verity LA*, *Poet's Choice*, *Lucky Jefferson*, *Poem Village*, and *What Rough Beast Covid 19 Edition*. *Tracing the Curve* is her first collection, Atmosphere Press.

EZEQUIEL NAYA, Buenos Aires, trained as a writer in the workshops of Diego Paszkowski and Fabián Casas before graduating from the Literary Creation masters from Universitat Pompeu Fabra. He is the author of *Fantasmas de Animales* (2012), published by Corregidor. He is a co-founder of Lata Peinada in Barcelona and Madrid.

CHRISTINE (CHRIS) NEUMAN holds a Masters in Creative Writing from Sacramento State University. She is largely influenced by James Tate, Allen Ginsberg, and Frank O'Hara. She has been published in *Cough Syrup*, *The Meadow*, and *¡Laplante!*. Chris enjoys cigarettes, Bob Dylan, and is learning to play guitar and harmonica.

AARON NOBES has most recently been published in *Andromeda Spaceways Magazine*, *Havik* and *Red Ogre Review*.

OKURA OF YAMA-NO-UE (c. 660 – 733) was a Japanese nobleman, envoy to Tang Dynasty China, and one of the major poets of the Man'yōshū, the oldest collection of Japanese poetry. His poems are often marked by his sympathy to common people, affection for children, and religious sincerity.

RAJENDRA PERSAUD is a poet and author. He lives with his beautiful wife Shaweta, loving daughter Aria, and dogs Coconut and Ethan. He is grateful for the opportunity to share his thoughts.

CANDICE PHELAN was born and raised in San Jose, CA.

Growing up, they discovered a love for creating things and strives to keep creating to this day through their hobbies. Candice is a senior at San Jose State University studying Creative Writing.

DAVID J.S. PICKERING is a native Oregonian, having grown up and lived much of his life in the working-class culture of the North Oregon Coast. He received the 2020 Airlie Prize for his first poetry collection, *Jesus Comes to Me as Judy Garland* (Airlie Press, 09/2021). His poetry is published in a variety of journals including *Reed Magazine, Pine Row, Raven Chronicles,* and *Gertrude Journal.* David never aspired to have a website, so he is a bit nonplussed to find that he now owns one, www.pickpoetry.com. David lives with his husband in Hillsboro, Oregon.

RICHARD PRINS is a New Yorker who has lived, worked, studied and recorded music in Dar es Salaam, and recipient of a 2023 PEN/ Heim Translation Fund Grant.

JAMES KELLY QUIGLEY is the winner of the Phyllis Smart-Young Prize in Poetry. Named among the 30 Below 30 list by *Narrative Magazine,* James is also a Pushcart Prize and two-time Best New Poets nominee. His manuscript *Aloneness* was a finalist for the Brittingham and Felix Pollak Prizes in Poetry (2022), as well as a semi-finalist for the Marystina Santiestevan First Book Prize (2022). Recent work has been published or is forthcoming in *The Los Angeles Review, New York Quarterly, Denver Quarterly, Dialogist, SLICE, The American Journal of Poetry,* and other places. He received both a BA and an MFA from New York University, where he taught undergraduate creative writing and was an editor of *Washington Square Review.* James was born and raised in New York. He works as a freelance writer in Brooklyn.

DELIA RADU is a journalist, writer and translator. Born and educated in Bucharest, she's lived and worked in London since 1999. Her journalistic work was published on the BBC News website and BBC Sounds. Her literary work has appeared in the *Cardinal Points Literary Journal, La Piccioletta Barca, Circumference* and *Sepia Quarterly.*

KUMAR PRANJAL RAI is a young Hindi poet from the city of Kannauj in Uttar Pradesh, India. His poems have appeared in a number of leading Hindi-language literary journals and magazines including

Vagarth, Kathadesh, Pakhi, Kathakram, Parikatha, Aksharparv,
and *Abhinav Imroz.* He daylights as a software professional and
competitive programmer.

CHANDRA RICE began writing as a child but never thought it
would lead anywhere. She had other plans for her future. It wasn't
until she was recruited to be a newspaper reporter that she began
writing professionally. It was a different kind of writing, but it
brought the joy back for her. Now, she writes for release, for therapy,
for fun, and for distraction.

YAN RONG served as scholar-in-residence at the Chinese/American
Association of Poetry and Poetics (CAA) at the Center for Programs
in Creative Writing at the University of Pennsylvania. He founded a
critical symposium at the Lakeside Poetry Club of Hangzhou Normal
University and is the author/editor of numerous books, including the
Anthology of the Wang Hongzhen Poetry.

THADDEUS RUTKOWSKI is the author of seven books, most
recently *Tricks of Light,* a poetry collection. He teaches at Medgar
Evers College and Columbia University and received a fiction writing
fellowship from the New York Foundation for the Arts.

LINDS SANDERS (she/her) is a multidisciplinary artist in
graduate school to learn where Clinical Mental Health Counseling
and art intersect. Her writing burrows in publications like *The Big
Issue, Plainsongs,* and *decomp.* Her artwork darts in and out of art
galleries as well as national/international publications such as *Gems
Zine, 3Elements, Harbor Review* and elsewhere. At the end of the
day all her work comes home to rest at LindsSanders.com and IG @
resounding_bell.

GEORGE SARANTARIS (1908-1941) was a Greek poet born in
Constantinople and raised in Italy. Over his lifetime, he composed
more than a thousand poems, developing a distinct poetic world that
evokes the sparse, light-filled Greek landscape. Sarantaris died in the
1940 Greco-Italian War tragically fighting against the country of his
upbringing, Italy.

JEFF SCHIFF is the author of *With light enough to braille me nextward*
(MAMMOTH books, 2023); *They: A Letter to America; That hum to
go by; Mixed Diction; Burro Heart; The Rats of Patzcuaro; The Homily*

of Infinitude; and *Anywhere in this Country*. Hundreds of his poems, essays, recordings, and photographs have appeared in more than one hundred and fifty publications worldwide. He has taught at Columbia College Chicago since 1987.

ELIZABETH SCHMERMUND is a poet, essayist, and scholar who lives in New York with her family. She has published in venues including *The Independent* and *Gyroscope Review*, among others, and her first chapbook is forthcoming from Finishing Line Press. She is an assistant professor in the English Department at SUNY Old Westbury.

MARK SCHMIDT is an English MA student currently studying at the University of South Dakota, and his poetry has been published in *Potpourri, Digging Through the Fat,* and *Train River Poetry*. He can be found on Instagram: @Poetry.In.My.Bones

HEIDI SEABORN is Executive Editor of *The Adroit Journal* and author of *Marilyn: Essays & Poems, [PANK]* Poetry Prize winner *An Insomniac's Slumber Party with Marilyn Monroe*, the acclaimed debut *Give a Girl Chaos* and Comstock Chapbook Award-winning *Bite Marks*. Recent work in *Blackbird, Beloit, Brevity, Copper Nickel, Cortland Review, diode, Financial Times of London, The Missouri Review, Penn Review, Radar, The Slowdown* and elsewhere. Heidi holds an BA from Stanford and an MFA from NYU.

EILEEN SEPULVEDA's love for writing began when she was just a teenager. Later, as a single mother of two boys, and working full time, she chose to go back to school and enrolled in Lehman College. She received her Bachelor of Arts degree as an English Honors student specializing in Creative Writing. She is the first in her family to receive such an honor. She was an editor and a contributor to the school newspaper, *Meridian*, writing articles that focused on the struggles and concerns of Lehman students and the larger Bronx community, including unfair policing, prison labor, and gentrification. Eileen writes poetry and short stories and will continue to work on a novel in progress.

RAVI SHANKAR, PhD is a Pushcart prize-winning poet, translator and professor who has published 15 books, including W.W. Norton's *Language for a New Century: Contemporary Poetry from the Middle East, Asia & Beyond*. He has appeared in such venues as *The New*

York Times, NPR, BBC and the PBS Newshour and won fellowships to the Corporation of Yaddo, Virginia Center for Creative Arts and the MacDowell Colony. He currently teaches creative writing at Tufts University and his memoir *Correctional*, called "the work of an absolutely brilliant writer," was published by University of Wisconsin Press in 2022.

ALICIA SHUPE is a 2nd year PhD at Illinois State University. She enjoys writing poetry, fiction, and some criticism. Her work can be seen in *Confluence*, *Cardinal Sins Magazine*, and the *Grassroots Writing Research Journal*. When she's not writing for publication, Alicia can be found watching online videos of huskies whose bark sounds like a human speaking.

SAM SIMON is a writer and translator from Oakland, CA. He is an associate editor for the *Barcelona Review* and teaches creative writing at the Institute for American Universities in Barcelona. He is a co-founder and managing editor of Infrasonica.org, a digital platform dedicated to non-Western sonic art and cultures. His translation of Naya's *Sueños del Atlántico* was published as *Ship of Dreams* in Mayday Magazine in 2021.

RANJITH SIVARAMAN is a poet from Kerala, a beautiful state in India. His poems merge nature imagery, human emotions, and human psychology into a gorgeous tapestry. Sivaraman's English poems are published in international literature magazines and journals from various locations like Alberta, Budapest, Essex, London, New York, Indiana, Lisbon, Colorado, California, and New Jersey, Tk'emlúpste Secwepemc, Kerala, Texas, Chennai & Toronto. His Poem "Shortest Distance" was released as a music video (https://youtu.be/qOLuHGiwNMU) in 2022. https://ranjithsivaraman.com

LIZZY SPARKS attends Ohio State, where she is majoring in English with a concentration in creative writing. She lives in southern Ohio. Thank you for considering my submission.

KYRA SPENCE's work has appeared or is forthcoming in New York's *Best Emerging Poets: An Anthology*, *Stirring: A Literary Collection*, *Pine Hills Review*, and elsewhere. She holds an MFA from the Iowa Writers' Workshop and teaches creative writing at the University of Iowa.

HRISHIKESH SRINIVAS is a graduate student in electrical engineering at Stanford University from Sydney, Australia. He was born in Chennai, India, and lived in Botswana during his early childhood years. His poems and translations have appeared in *UNSWeetened Literary Journal, Otoliths, Meniscus*, and *Mantis*. He was awarded the Dorothea Mackellar National Poetry Award in 2011, and the Nillumbik Ekphrasis Poetry Youth Award in 2013, also being included in the *Laughing Waters Road: Art, Landscape and Memory in Eltham* 2016 exhibition catalogue.

ALEX STANLEY is a graduate of Boston College, and he received his MFA in Creative Writing at the University of California, Irvine. He is a former sports journalist, and his sports writing has been featured in *Sports Illustrated*. His published poems have appeared in *American Poets Magazine, HCE Review, Poet's Choice, Helix Magazine, Sunspot Literary Journal, RockPaperPoem, Limit Experience Journal, Beyond Words Magazine, Wingless Dreamer, Clepsydra Literary and Art Magazine, Wild Roof Journal, The Closed Eye Open, Quibble, Duck Lake Journal, The Write Launch, Doozine*, and *Hare's Paw Literary Journal*. He is a recipient of the 2021 Academy of American Poets Award. He resides in Costa Mesa, CA.

CORRIE THOMPSON is a poet and photographer from the suburbs outside Chicago. Her writing appears in *Eclectica Magazine, Good Life Literary Journal, Haiku Journal*, and *Flash Fiction Magazine*. She would love to become a birch tree in her next life and be one with the natural world she loves so much. Her instagram is @mis.underwood.

Originally from a sunny island in Southeast Asia, SHER TING is a Singaporean-Chinese currently residing in Australia. She is a 2021 Writeability Fellow with Writers Victoria and a 2021 Pushcart and Best of The Net nominee with work published/forthcoming in *Pleiades, The Journal, The Pinch, Salamander, Chestnut Review, Rust+Moth, The Citron Review* and elsewhere. Her debut chapbook, *Bodies of Separation*, is forthcoming with Cathexis Northwest Press, while her second chapbook, *The Long-Lasting Grief of Foxes*, is forthcoming with CLASH! Books in 2023. She tweets at @sherttt and writes at sherting.carrd.co

RUTH TOWNE is a graduate of the Stonecoast MFA program.

Her work has recently appeared in *WOMEN. LIFE.*, a special issue of *Beyond Words Literary Magazine*, and *Monsoons: A Collection of Poetry* by Poet's Choice Publishing. She has forthcoming publications with Black Spot Books, Inlandia Publishing, NiftyLit, and Drunk Monkeys.

KYRA TRUMBULL is majoring in English as a freshman at Colgate University. She is an aspiring writer from New Jersey and greatly enjoys composing poems while walking around campus.

PETER URKOWITZ lives in Salem, Massachusetts, where he works in a college library. He has published poems and art in *Meat for Tea: The Valley Review*, *Oddball Magazine*, *Sextant*, *Molecule*, and the *Lily Poetry Review*. His *Fake Zodiac Signs* chapbook was published by Meat for Tea Press in 2020.

EMILY WAN is a scholar of premodern Japanese literature whose research focuses on renga (medieval Japanese linked verse) as an intersection of literary and social practice. She graduated from Stanford University in 2022 with a degree in East Asian Studies (Japan) and Translation Studies minor and is now a Fulbright Fellow at Waseda University. Current research includes a study of renga in modern Japan and a project on the place of rules in the poet Sōgi's renga.

PAMELA WAX is the author of *Walking the Labyrinth* (Main Street Rag, 2022) and the chapbook, *Starter Mothers* (Finishing Line Press, 2023). Her poems have received a Best of the Net nomination and awards from *Crosswinds*, *Paterson Literary Review*, *Poets' Billow*, *Oberon*, and the Robinson Jeffers Tor House. She has been published in literary journals including *Barrow Street*, *Tupelo Quarterly*, *About Place Journal*, *Rust & Moth*, *Mudfish*, *Nimrod*, *Connecticut River Review*, *Naugatuck River Review*, *Sixfold*, and *Passengers Journal*. An ordained rabbi, Pam offers spirituality and poetry workshops online from her home in the Northern Berkshires of Massachusetts.

EMMA WELLS is a mother and English teacher. She has poetry published with various literary journals and magazines. She enjoys writing flash fiction and short stories also. Her debut novel, *Shelley's Sisterhood*, is forthcoming.

SHANNA WILLIAMS (she/her) lives in San Francisco, CA. When

she's not breaking her own heart and writing about it, she's usually drinking red wine in a fuzzy robe.

ANNA WRIGHT is currently a high school senior at a small private school in the Northeastern Pennsylvania region and have been writing poetry for just under three years.

KENTON K. YEE recently placed poetry in *Constellations*, *Plume Poetry*, *The Threepenny Review*, *The Indianapolis Review*, *Tipton Poetry Journal*, *Hollins Critic*, and *Pembroke Magazine*, among others. A Stanford graduate (JD'00, MA'00, and PhD'01), Iowa Summer Poetry Workshop alumnus, and former Columbia University faculty member, he writes from northern California.

Printed and bound by CPI Group (UK) Ltd, Croydon, CR0 4YY

13/04/2025

14656450-0001